MODERN DAY
TROJAN
HORSE

The Islamic Doctrine of Immigration
Accepting Freedom or Imposing Islam?

SAM SOLOMON & E AL MAQDISI

ANM
publishers

D0179631

MODERN DAY TROJAN HORSE
Al-Hijra: The Islamic Doctrine of Immigration
Accepting Freedom or Imposing Islam?

BY SAM SOLOMON & E AL MAQDISI

ISBN: 978-0-9794929-5-2 Paperback

Published by:

Advancing Native Missions
P.O. Box 5303
Charlottesville, VA 22905
www.Adnamis.org

PUBLISHER'S NOTE: *The authors of this book have employed British usage regarding spelling and punctuation.*

CONTENTS

PREFACE

The meaning of *Al-Hijra* is 'to immigrate', and the Islamic calendar starts with that date, i.e., the date Muhammad 'immigrated' from Mecca to Medina, for which he had planned carefully and meticulously laying down the groundwork for the Islamic State, soon to grow after his death into a formidable empire ruled by the laws and regulations laid out by him, called the *Shariah*.

The *Hijra* was enshrined by Muhammad from the outset within Islam as the 'Doctrine of Immigration', or the 'peaceful' means of extending the Islamic political state garbed and girded in religious terminology. *Hijra* and military conquest are two components of Islamic expansion.

So today as we see staggering numbers of immigrants from Muslim countries in Europe and in the Americas, with developing Muslim communities that are self-segregating and asking for more and more rights and privileges to the point of the recent adoption of *Shariah* Family Law in the United Kingdom — we have to ask the questions as in the title of this book, "Are these communities wanting to join the free societies? Or, are they extending the 'Abode of Islam' as per the 'Doctrine of Immigration' which was modeled by Muhammad in the initial *Hijra?*"

But we are getting ahead of ourselves. Let us take a look at traditional 'immigration' as we have experienced it in the past, and see how today's egregious demands of Muslim immigrant communities match up.

Free immigration by various groups to Western Europe and the Americas has long been a welcome part of national growth, as immigrants were searching primarily for opportunities for a better life and were quick to identify with their host nations and so to contribute their talents to the national good.

While the 'forced' immigration through the slave trade of the 18th and 19th centuries, mainly from Western Africa to North and South America, was a serious blemish in the development of the countries involved, but thanks to the dedicated efforts of men of good will, strong Christian convictions and belief in human rights, the era of slavery became past history, with the former slaves having become by now fully free citizens and with influence in all aspects of the political, economic and social life. Yes, there are and continue to be, injustices, social and economic imbalances. But the democratic 'system' has succeeded in bringing the needed reforms.

The developments over the past 20-30 years in Europe and the USA have witnessed a great influx of new immigrants — from cheap labour, to students seeking college degrees, to immigrants simply seeking a better life. In the UK and other European countries, immigrants from former colonies came in large numbers to take on lower paying jobs, thus aiding in the economic growth of Europe.

So why does this book focus on the subject of 'Islamic Immigration?' Why should this be an issue at all? After all, aren't the Muslim immigrants just like any other immigrants from China, the Indian subcontinent or Africa? After all, these other immigrants try to preserve their ethnic identity and even form lobby groups to fend for their rights and special requirements.

'Ethnic Separatism' has been dubbed as the effort by ethnic minorities to derive special consideration within the political and social framework of the host country or state. These vary from simple matters like demands for observance of religious holidays, to the allowance for developing a form of a separate identity, up to the extreme of political separation into separate states. By and large, this has consistently been a defensive form aimed at preserving the group's identity, whether it is linguistic, national, religious, and so on.

The authors of this book argue that 'Islamic Immigration' (*Al-Hijra*, in Arabic) is tied organically and inseparably to a form of immigration which is an integral part of the Islamic call (*da'wa*) to establish an

Islamic state or political power base and to spread Islam. There are two equally important starting points to this assertion:

1. Islam owes its political, social and economic expansion to the migration of Muhammad in the year 622 AD from Mecca to Yathrib[1], a city to the North of Mecca reachable in a few days' journey at that time.

2. The Islamic religion is based for the most part on the full application of the *Sunnah*, which is the following of Muhammad's example to the fullest extent.

The casual reader may say, 'So what?'

The authors bring to light that these two points guided and supported the operative and strategic mechanisms for implementing (a) what Muslims believe universally: that Islam is Allah's only religion (Sura 3:19) and (b) that in the words of its founder, "Islam is exalted and nothing is exalted above it."

Islamic history points out that Muhammad during his 13 years in Mecca had very limited success, but after the *Hijra*, and in less than 10 years, he became the undisputed ruler and prophet of all of Arabia, ready to march onward to take on the two empires to the north and to the west of Arabia: the Roman and Persian Empires, respectively. The Islamic calendar starts with the *Hijra* for this and other reasons.

The authors provide the painstaking detail of how the *Hijra* was not a sudden desperate attempt by Muhammad and his followers to flee Mecca for a better life in Medina. In fact it was a methodically planned event whereby Muhammad used his shrewd political manoeuvring and leadership skills to transform every development into an advantage without losing his focus on the final goal. In the process he unified the pagan Arabs as Muslims and placed the Jewish and Christian Arabs in a subservient condition. Prior to becoming subservient

---

[1] Muhammad quickly renamed Yathrib "Al-Madina Al-Munawwarah" (City of Lights), or "Madinat Ul Nabi" (City of the prophet) or simply "Madina."

they were masters in their own towns and oases. More importantly, Muhammad developed a 'model' to be emulated by generations to come — for 1400 years and still counting!

This model is called the 'Doctrine of Immigration,' and it provides the mechanisms and processes to be followed by dedicated and pious Muslims to transform the world into the abode of Islam. And since the *Sunnah* requires these pious Muslims to follow the example of Muhammad, the Doctrine of Immigration is applicable for all places and all times — only to be updated and regulated by the 'Men of Knowledge' (the *Ulama*), who are entrusted in adapting the *Fiqh* (Islamic Jurisprudence) outworking to changing times and conditions. And although Islam during Muhammad's time and for many years later spread by means of military expansion ('Islamic *Futuhat*'), many existing Islamic societies/countries have been gained through 'immigration;' societies/countries such as Indonesia, Malaysia, East Africa, West Africa, parts of India, central Asia, and so on.

Modern Islamic intellectuals and planners have been actively working on applying the Doctrine of Immigration to the Muslim societies in Europe, North America, and Latin America. The advocated mechanisms and tools are not mere 'parallels' of what Muhammad did in Medina some 1400 years ago, but actually are precise imitations and applications of what he did and developed, as you will see in this book.

If this is the case, as demonstrated by one example after the other, then does the image of a 'Trojan Horse' apply? In Greek history, the Trojan horse was a brilliant stratagem by the Athenians after failing to breach the Trojan walls. Leaving the horse as a "gift", they gave the appearance of lifting the siege, but Athenian fighters had remained within the statue, only to emerge later. Thus the "Trojan horse" has come to mean any measure that looks innocent, and obscures true intent. Is Islamic immigration then a deceptive effort to take over Western societies while they are unaware? The authors point to the gradual attempts to spread Islamic influence in small steps, but with the aim of making Islamic Shariah laws fully functional.

Aside from the fact that *Shariah* laws by themselves are antiquated and incompatible with modern and universally accepted values and freedoms, by placing them on a par with the laws of the host countries a two-tier legal system is bound to emerge. Have Western democracies struggled for many centuries to establish the principle of the separation of Church and State, only now to be drawn into the merging of the mosque with the State? All of a sudden, state schools in the UK (and public schools that only recently banned 'prayer' as an intrusion against this doctrine) are now more than happy to provide not only ablution and prayer facilities to Muslim students but also time allowances to practice the prayers at the appointed times — to provide just one example.

The ultimate cause for concern, however, is the antiquated doctrine of human rights and freedom of religion and expression in Islam. Islam, after all, considers non-Muslims as apostates (*kafirs*) with lesser rights than Muslims. Freedom of religion in Islam is only one way: a non-Muslim is free to become a Muslim, but not the other way around. As for freedom of expression, Islamic pressure groups at the highest levels are working hard at writing legislation and international agreements that consider any criticism of Islam as a 'hate crime'.

The answers to this dilemma are not easy. Western free societies should not compromise on their values by imposing artificial controls on Muslims. On the contrary, Muslims need to have the opportunity to have free choice, much like Christians and secular people who make their decisions on their worldviews through study and introspection outside the pressures of the community or family. Muslims need to be in a position to question the alleged 'truth claims' of Islam. Thanks to the media and to the free societies of the West, tens, perhaps hundreds of thousands of Muslims have in the past 20 years or so, opted out of Islam and found richer spiritual and moral lives. Simultaneously, *Shariah* laws need to be seriously curtailed.

It is hoped that the astute reader and researcher would examine this book carefully and relate it to what is happening on the ground.

It is also hoped that through deeper thoughts and introspections, some imaginatively creative and practically effective solutions to the 'immigration doctrine of Islam' would emerge, solutions that are genuine, lovingly Christian and highly sympathetic to the plight of the Muslims inside their Trojan horse who want to opt out of that role.

Gideon
November, 2008

ENDORSEMENT BY GEERT WILDERS

In 2006, Libyan leader Moammar Khadafi made it very clear in a speech to thousands of people: "We have fifty million Muslims in Europe. There are signs that Allah will grant Islam victory in Europe — without swords, without guns, without conquests. The fifty million Muslims of Europe will turn it into a Muslim continent within a few decades."

So one can see that the threat from Islam doesn't just come in the form of Islamic terrorism by suicide bombers trying to wreak havoc in our cities. More often, it comes in the form of a gradual and incremental transformation of our societies and legal systems, or what is termed 'Islamisation' of our democratic societies by the vast growing numbers of Muslim immigrants who are importing Islam into our Western way of life.

Many in the West do not see the dangers that Islamisation poses to our civilization. Especially the ruling elite, who refuse to take action to counter Islamisation by prohibiting *Sharia* Law, or to take measures to regulate mass immigration.

Blinded by political correctness and their ideals of cultural relativism, they are giving in to increasing demands by Muslim communities. That is a costly mistake, because Islam is not compatible with our Western civilization nor will it ever be. That's because Islam doesn't want to coexist; it wants to set the agenda.

We cannot afford to be in a state of denial much longer. We have to defend our freedom. We owe that to our children, to ourselves and to our ancestors who fought long and hard for our freedom and made our lives so much more prosperous and safe.

In *Modern Day Trojan Horse*, Sam Solomon & E Al Maqdisi give an excellent insider view of how immigration is a *bona fide* doctrine of Islam, not just a random immigration of people looking for jobs, opportunities, and a better life — and thus is being used, as set in motion by Muhammad, as a vital strategy of conquest. They explain how and why immigration is going under the radar, and how the demands of the growing Muslim communities are transforming our society.

Solomon is a genius. I don't know anyone with the knowledge, perseverance and strength of argument such as that of Solomon.

I hope that every person in the Western world reads it, including the sleeping political elite. This book should bring about a much needed awakening.

If this book does not serve as an eye-opener for even the most convinced cultural relativist, nothing will.

Geert Wilders MP
Voorzitter Tweede Kamerfractie Partij voor de Vrijheid (PVV)
Chairman Party for Freedom (PVV)

DEDICATION

It is not the Muslim individual as a neighbour that we are opposed to, it is the mounting Islamic demand on behalf of growing self-segregated communities within non-Muslim nations, all over the world, for the institution of a legal system that rejects allegiance to any national state, or allegiance to any world view other than that of Islam.

The earliest voice sounding the alarm of increasing immigration, self-segregation, and resulting political influence of Muslims in non-Muslim lands was, and is, an Egyptian-born Jewish scholar by the name of Bat Ye'or. She has spent decades researching the past to predict the future in regard to how Islam swallowed up whole societies the first time around, from the 7th century till today. This was accomplished either by waging war in the classic sense – Jihad by the sword – or through the force of numbers that is immigrating and building segregated Muslim communities in the host countries, reducing the host communities to Dhimmitude status, in increments.

Bat Ye'or's latest book, Eurabia: The Euro-Arab Axis, as well as her other books on the topic, detailing the historical precedent, mechanisms and intent of Islam, culminates with a mere description of facts on the ground at this point in time, particularly in the European Union, and the Americas. We applaud her for her scholarship, her tenacity, and her passion for truth and freedom—which has in turn laid a groundwork of credibility for those who follow in her footsteps.

Standing up against the politically correct voices of compromise in Europe, giving way to fear, resulting in the acceptance of Dhimmi status, where freedom of speech, belief, and conscience are the first casualties.

We dedicate this work to Bat Ye'or.

In the United Kingdom… we dedicate this book:

To Baroness Caroline Cox and Professor John Marks, for their boldness, courageous publications and outspokenness on this matter;

To Dr Patrick Sookhdeo for remaining dedicated to the cause, defying conventional wisdom, and who predicted long ago the demographic changes and its dangers when there was nothing on the horizon;

To Melanie Phillips for keeping the uncomfortable realities in the public eye without fear through the might of her pen.

In Europe… we dedicate it to Geert Wilders for fighting tyranny. Fearlessly continuing to put public interest above personal gain while under threat, and while facing mounting opposition.

Last, but not least, to every defender of our Judeo-Christian heritage.

Sam Solomon & Elias Al Maqdisi

ACKNOWLEDGEMENTS

We the authors acknowledge inexpressible gratitude to all those who stood with us and held our hands through their faithful intercessions, which kept us focused.

Our thanks to those who have read and commented on this book. It was their criticism that enhanced this document.

Our deepest thanks to all those provided and supported us through this hard journey.

May you all be rewarded beyond your wildest expectations.

The Authors

FOREWORD

Sam Solomon and E. Al·Maqdisi, *Modern Day Trojan Horse — Al-Hijra: The Islamic Doctrine of Immigration, Accepting freedom or imposing Islam?* November 2008

Sam Solomon and E. Al Maqdisi have provided the general Western public a valuable service in publishing this book. Based on their intimate knowledge of the Islamic source scriptures, they have set out the contemporary relevance of the Islamic doctrine of migration (*Hijra*), based on Muhammad's example, that has always been linked to the wider Islamic *jihad* ideology: the effort by every means possible to expand the political, religious and cultural hegemony of Islam in new territories.

While accepting that many Muslims migrate to the West for economic and personal reasons, the authors clearly show how the very nature of Islamic doctrine, tradition, practice, religious establishment, and ideology tend to shape the initially amorphous migrants into a segregated community that challenges the non-Muslim political and cultural systems in their new countries of residence. Islamisation of the host society will be the inevitable outcome of this process.

Muslims in the West face the choice of two different responses to their situation as a minority. Depending on their view of the *Hijra* and its level of significance as a model for today; either Muslim minorities can decide that their goal is integration into their host societies or they can accept the *Hijra* model advocated by Islamists, and consider their community in the West as a bridgehead for the expansion of *Dar al-Islam* (the House of Islam).

Plans to Islamise the West invariably refer to Muhammad's staged *Hijra* model as the paradigm to be emulated today, and develop various stages needed to attain the goal. The right moment to move to the phase of power arrives when the Islamic movement is strong enough to overturn the existing non-Muslim government and replace it with an Islamic one. Requests for concessions from Muslim minorities should be assessed in the light of the *Hijra* concept.

Migration includes the potential use of both peaceful and violent means. A recent article in the *Le Monde diplomatique*, has this to say about the relevance of Muhammad's migration paradigm for today's violent jihadists:

> Two points are key to understanding jihadist culture. Travelling to a foreign land for jihad is often described as a migration or *Hijra* in Arabic. The same term is used for the flight of Mohammad and his companions from Mecca to Medina in 622AD, which is central to Islam and marks the beginning of the Muslim calendar. For jihadists, to go to Afghanistan or Iraq is a mystical experience comparable to the journey of the Prophet and his companions. Many jihadist militants, such as Abu Hamza al-Muhajer, Zarqawi's alleged successor in Iraq, take the *nom de guerre muhajer*, which means "migrant". The second powerful myth is that of the destruction of an empire by a handful of lightly armed youths – made possible only by a mystical dimension.
>
> (*Vicken Cheterian, "The Iraq generation", Le* Monde diplomatique, *English edition, December 2008*)

The effects of the compulsory example of Muhammad's *Hijra* and its mystical effect on his contemporary followers are being felt today all around the globe.

This book sounds a clear warning note as to the predictable outcome of the contemporary Muslim migration to the West. All those concerned with the preservation of the Judeo-Christian culture, the rule of law, equality, individual rights, and religious freedom should take note.

Dr. Patrick Sookhdeo
December 2008

INTRODUCTION

The recent announcement by the British Government of empowering and legalising UK *Shariah* Courts has alarmed a lot of people who have begun to inquire as to how this could be possible? This has especially been so when it came to light that the *Shariah* courts have been running within the Muslim community in the UK for years prior to this official endorsement by the Ministry of Justice.

The real question is: *how can a minority make such inroads so successfully into such an established system?* What are the real reasons for this alternative system? Why would people migrate here in the first place, if they wanted to live under a different legal system? Would it not be much better for them to stay put in their own countries? And naturally there are many more similar questions along these lines!

To understand the demand for *Shariah* courts in the UK and other European countries, one has to look into a major aspect of it — the overall Islamic doctrine of immigration; that the Muslim migration to the West particularly, and to the free world generally, is for a purpose set by Islamic ideology. The roots stem from the Qur'an and the *Sunnah*.

The whole issue of Muslim immigration cannot be understood without understanding the *Hijra*, or "Doctrine of Immigration," and the other doctrines related to it. For the modern-day Muslim migration is rooted in and tightly knitted with the migration of Muhammad from Mecca to Medina.

MUHAMMAD'S ORIGINAL MIGRATION

Muhammad's *Hijra*, or migration from Mecca to Medina, is considered to be notably the most important Islamic event and is exemplified by the fact that the Islamic calendar starts with that event. For *Hijra* changed the status of Islam as a religion and of the Muslims as a community, transforming them from being a weak people to a powerful political entity, from being scattered groups of loyal individuals into a consolidated army, a united community and ultimately into a powerful socio–religious political state.

The most important outcome of the *Hijra* (migration of Muhammad from Mecca to Medina) was the spread of Islam outside and beyond the bounds of Mecca, not only as a religion but a combined, socio-religious and socio-political system. That is why *Hijra* is considered to be the most important method of spreading Islam as a way of life, meaningful religion, and a political system and consolidating it far beyond the Muslim countries.

Hence, *Hijra*, as an example set up by the prophet of Islam, must be imitated and emulated by all Muslims 'as a religious obligation.'

The Example of the Prophet

The example of Muhammad is known as the *Sunnah* and is regarded as an equal to the Qur'an as the primary source of the *Shariah*. In fact without the *Sunnah* there can be no Islam at all. For a Muslim's life is governed more by the *Sunnah* than it is by the Qur'an. Almost all practical outworking of the Islamic religion is based on the literal following of what Muhammad did, said, or approved.

Sunnah is an Arabic word meaning 'to set, to form or to shape'; in this case it is known as *Sunnatu-A'nnabi,* meaning 'the example of the Prophet'.

The *Sunnah* was officially and appropriately established in Medina. The fledgling Muslim community was a heterogeneous community made of Arab tribes from Mecca (called *Al-Muhajiroon,* meaning 'the Immigrants,' the Aws and Khazraj tribes from Medina (called, *Al-Ansar*) meaning 'the victorious guardians' (of the Immigrants) and others.

Within a short period after Muhammad's *Hijra,* tribal conflicts emerged as each tribe had long traditions that were at variance with the other tribes — even though they had all accepted Islam as their religion with Muhammad as its prophet. Muhammad quickly discovered what would become a major explosive situation. Hence, he asked all the tribes to drop their ancestral practices and adopt a spirit of a new 'Islamic' community and to drop all consideration of their traditions prior to Islam[2]. As a result, he required all Muslims to follow his 'example' in all aspects of behaviour and all of that was confirmed in a long series of 'Qur'anic' injunctions — being the direct words of Allah revealed to Muhammad in a variety of ways. Here are some of those injunctions:

> Sura 68:4 "And verily, you (O Muhammad) are on an exalted standard of character." (In other words a divine command to the faithful to take him as a model by for their lives.)
>
> Sura 53:2–5 "Your companion (Muhammad) has neither gone astray nor has erred. Nor does he speak of (his own) desire. It is only an Inspiration that is inspired. He has been taught by one mighty in power."

Now these Qur'anic injunctions to follow Muhammad were taken completely literally, i.e. Muhammad used them to require Muslims to

---

[2] To support this case, Muhammad declared that all traditions prior to Islam were in the 'Period of Ignorance' (in Arabic, *'Asr Al-Jahiliah*)

follow everything he said and did. This went into the minutest details such as methods of washing, how to grow one's beard, or even how to enter a bathroom. Even when someone did something that gained Muhammad's approval this became part of the *Sunnah*.

Of course, there were those who said that they only desired the life after. In this case Allah 'revealed' that they must follow Muhammad and imitate his example as recorded in Sura 33:21,

> "Indeed in the Messenger of Allah you have a good example to follow for him who hopes in (the Meeting with) Allah and the Last Day and remembers Allah much."

Some of the new converts were still hesitant to strictly follow Muhammad and his example and they said that all they wanted was to be obedient only unto Allah. So Muhammad claimed to have now received Sura 4:80,

> "He **who obeys the Messenger** (Muhammad), has indeed **already obeyed Allah**".

He went even further to say that their allegiance to him was an allegiance to Allah as in Sura 48:10,

> "Verily, those **who give pledge to you (O Muhammad) they are giving pledge to Allah**. The Hand of Allah is over their hands. Then whosoever breaks his pledge, breaks only to his own harm, and whosoever fulfills what he has covenanted with Allah, He will bestow on him a great reward".

Henceforth, in all new revelations Allah and Muhammad were paired together, both legislating with equal power:

> Sura 33:36 "It is not for a believer, man or woman, when **Allah and His Messenger** have decreed a matter that they should have any option in their decision. **And whoever disobeys Allah and His Messenger**, he has indeed strayed in a plain error".

Also,

> Sura 9:29 "Fight against those who believe not in Allah, nor in the Last Day, nor forbid that which has been forbidden by **Allah and His Messenger** and those who acknowledge not the religion of truth, among the people of the Scripture (Jews and Christians), until they pay the *Jizyah* with willing submission, and feel themselves subdued."

Just believing in Allah was not sufficient, to be a true believer one had to be a firm believer in Muhammad and his finality and even this was now a revealed Qur'anic passage:

> Sura 24:62 "The true believers are only those, who believe in (the Oneness of) **Allah and His Messenger** (Muhammad),"
>
> Sura 49:15 "Only those are the believers who have believed in **Allah and His Messenger**, and afterward doubt not but strive with their wealth and their lives for the Cause of Allah. Those! They are the truthful."

Now it was revealed that the owners of all things were and are both Allah and his messenger Muhammad as everything else belongs to Allah and his messenger:

> Sura 8:1 "They ask you (O Muhammad) about the spoils of war. Say: 'The spoils are for **Allah and His Messenger**'. So fear Allah and adjust all matters of difference among you, and **obey Allah and His Messenger if you are believers**".

But soon Allah changed and granted Muhammad all the authority and from henceforth Muhammad was to grant and forbid, to give and withhold whatever he thought to be appropriate as per Sura 59:7,

> "What Allah gave as booty to His Messenger from the people of the townships, — it is for Allah, His Messenger,

the kindred (of Messenger Muhammad), the orphans, (the poor), and the wayfarer, in order that it may not become a fortune used by the rich among you. And **whatsoever the Messenger gives you, take it, and whatsoever he forbids you, abstain (from it)**, and fear Allah. Verily, Allah is Severe in punishment".

In other words Muhammad's authority was now beyond the text of the Qur'an itself. Muslims were told that any vexing of Muhammad was equivalent to blasphemy and his rights and sanctity were equal to that of Allah and above.

Furthermore, Muhammad's authority was not only in matters of the world but was to be extended to the hereafter:

Sura 4:59 "O you who believe! **Obey Allah and obey the Messenger**" As mercy depended on the true obedience of Allah and his messenger, but even that was to change.

Sura 3:132 "And **obey Allah and the Messenger** (Muhammad) that you may obtain mercy."

Now compare it with the next verse:

Sura 24:56 "And perform Prayers (As-Salat), and give alms (Zakat) and **obey the Messenger (Muhammad) that you may obtain mercy.**"

Almost all Islamic practises are from *Sunnah* and none of them are recorded in the Qur'an. For example the prayer call known as *Azan* comes from *Sunnah*, the prayer details of how many rounds each time and the details of how to pray, as well as the details of how to do ablution, etc. comes from *Sunnah*.

The *Hajj* or pilgrimage and its details, the dress code, the Muslim cap, and all other details of one's day-to-day activities are deduced from *Sunnah*. So the authority of Muhammad in Islam is virtually absolute. He is the centre of it all, thus Muslims are required to follow him, imitate him, and emulate him in all things and every aspect of their lives. For a Muslim *Sunnah* is the very word of Allah.

In this case his example of *Hijra* or migration is an obligatory duty on Muslims for the enhancement and the advance of Islam. Ibn Taymiyya[3] sums it up well when he says that the right of Allah and the right of his apostle are forever paired together, for the sanctity of Allah and his apostle are one, and they are inseparable. Whosoever vexes the prophet vexes Allah, whosoever obeys the apostle has already obeyed Allah himself. This *Ummah* has no link between any of its members and their Lord except through the messenger, there is no other method, they have no purpose without him; **for Allah has set Muhammad in his own place**, to command, to forbid, to reveal and to disclose. So it is not possible to differentiate between Allah and his apostle in any of these matters.

---

[3] يقول ابن تيمية في كتابه : الصارم والمسلول على شاتم الرسول ص
40-41: حق الله وحق رسوله متلازمان : " ان جهة حرمة الله تعالى ورسوله جهة واحدة ؛ فمن آذى الرسول فقد آذى الله ،
ومن أطاعه فقد أطاع الله؛ لأن الأمة لا يصلون ما بينهم وبين ربهم الا بواسطة الرسول ، ليس لأحد منهم طريق غيره ولا
سبب سواه، وقد أقامه الله مقام نفسه في أمره ونهيه وأخباره وبيانه، فلا يجوز ان يفرق بين الله ورسوله في شيء من هذه
الامور

Ibn Taymiyya states in his book "Assaarim wal Maslool 'ala Shaatem Arrasoul, PP 40-41, "Allah's rights and the Messenger's rights are equivalent. The direction for facing and obeying Allah is the same as that of facing and obeying Muhammad. Whoever insults the Messenger insults Allah, and whoever obeys the Messenger then he has already obeyed Allah, because the members of the Islamic "Ummah" cannot connect with their creator except through the Messenger. No one has a means to Allah except through the Messenger, and Allah has placed (Muhammad) in his stead in all matters for commanding and forbidding and explaining, and it is not allowed to make a distinction between Allah and his Messenger in any of these matters.

FORMS OF
ISLAMIC MIGRATION

There may be many various reasons why people migrate from one location to another, be it local, or from one country to another. But here we are only concerned and focused on a particular type of Islamic immigration: that which is set in motion for the sake of the advancement of Islam. Islamic migration can be internal from one location or city to another or from one local district to another; it could be from one university to another if the Islamic leaders make that known as a need in that area to aid and consolidate that particular Muslim community. Once a location has been taken over and Islam consolidated, volunteers are asked to consider moving to another location in order to strengthen a fledging Muslim community and raise higher the banner of Islam. This is because immigration is legally binding on all Muslims, especially on those who are able to implement it. In other words, Islamically speaking, migration is not limited to being from country to country only, but even within the same office building, for the reasons just explained.

Muhammad's immigration to Medina provided him with a conducive environment in the sense that now he had much more freedom than when he was in Mecca. In Mecca he and his followers were under surveillance, in Medina he was completely free to do whatever he wanted. He had his own headquarters now established in his Medina mosque, which he utilised to prepare, to mobilise and to organise himself and his followers to launch attacks on his enemies. This was the case, both in Medina, to where he had migrated and made his new home against his host community, as well as in Mecca, where he had migrated from, ultimately subduing them all. Therefore, immigration is viewed as a transitional period of preparation for transforming the host society from an open, or non-Muslim, society into an Islamic society or at least one where Islam would be supreme. From this newly gained position they may even be able to affect the country of origin as Muhammad did.

Just like the great commission of the New Testament where the Risen Lord Jesus charged his disciples to go into the whole world and proclaim the good news of the Kingdom, Muhammad did something similar. As the Qur'an declares in Sura 3:83,

"Do they seek for other than the Religion of Allah?-while all creatures in the heavens and on earth have, willing or unwilling, bowed to His Will (accepted Islam), and to Him shall they all be brought back,"

This surrender to Allah in Islam must be achieved by all and every means possible, just as the verse states willingly or unwillingly. With this goal in mind together with the methodology of its achievement by Muhammad the prophet of Islam proclaimed:

"I charge you with five of what Allah has charged me with: to assemble, to listen, to obey, to immigrate and to wage Jihad for the sake of Allah[4]."

So *Hijra* or migration is binding on all Muslims for numerous reasons; the most important being that migration is preparatory to *jihad* with an aim and objective of securing victory for Islam and Muslims either in another country or generally as a community.

As illustrated in Fig. 1 all the five Islamic pillars are there to inspire and encourage the believers to take the cause of Allah forward in *jihad*. The *jihad* may vary. It may be outright war or it may take a different tactic, but here we are considering the *jihad of migration* and how it is achieved by explaining the Islamic doctrines it is rooted in.

Each of these five directives – to assemble, to listen, to obey, to migrate, and to wage *jihad* for the sake of Allah have been elaborated on by Muslim scholars and turned into systematic doctrines.

---

[4] Hadith no 2863 Kitab al Amthael reported by Tirmizi, also reported by Imam Ahmed Ibn Hanbel as Hadith no 17344

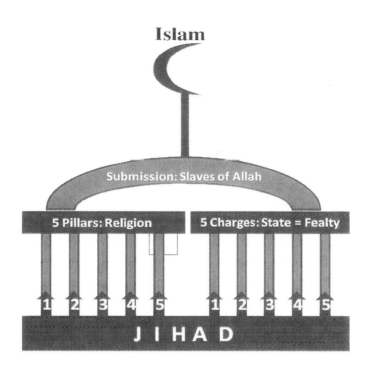

Figure 1: The Jihad Doctrine is the foundation of both inseparable components of Islam: Religion and State. The 5 Pillars are: (1) The Shahada (Testimony to Allah and Muhammad), (2) Salat (prayer), (3) Sawm (fasting), (4) Zakat (Religious tax), and (5) Hajj (Pilgrimage to Mecca). The five charges are: (1) to assemble, (2) to listen, (3) to obey, (4) to migrate and (5) to wage jihad. Note that according to other sources of Islamic jurisprudence, Jihad is all-encompassing and that is why it is shown as the foundation in this figure. Note that in Islam 'submission,' is the submission of a slave to his master.

1. **To Assemble:** (*Tajammo'h*) comes from the word *jama'a* the same root as the word 'mosque' meaning assemble or gather. In this case it is to join a Muslim community. To be part of it, one has to believe in Allah and his messenger — namely Muhammad who was sent as the "last and final prophet to mankind." In the following Qur'anic verses note the use of the phrase "those who believed" as the starting point or link to what follows.

Sura 2:218 "Verily, those who have believed, and those who have emigrated (for Allah's Religion) and have striven hard in the Way of Allah, all these hope for Allah's Mercy. And Allah is Oft-Forgiving, Most-Merciful."

Sura 8:72 "Verily, those who believed, and emigrated and strove hard and fought with their property and their lives in the Cause of Allah as well as those who gave (them) asylum and help, — these are (all) allies to one another. And as to those who believed but did not emigrate (to you, O Muhammad), you owe no duty of protection to them until they emigrate, but if they seek your help in religion, it is your duty to help them except against a people with whom you have a treaty of mutual alliance, and Allah is the All-Seer of what you do."

Sura 8:74–75 "And those who believed, and emigrated and strove hard in the Cause of Allah (*Al-Jihad*), as well as those who gave (them) asylum and aid; — these are the believers in truth, for them is forgiveness and a generous provision, i.e. (Paradise) And those who believed afterwards, and emigrated and strove hard along with you, (in the Cause of Allah) they are of you. But kindred by blood are nearer to one another regarding inheritance in the decree ordained by Allah. Verily, Allah is the All-Knower of everything."

Sura 9:20 "Those who believed and emigrated and strove hard and fought in Allah's Cause with their wealth and their lives are far higher in degree with Allah. They are the successful."

Gathering obviously requires mosques, or simply beginning in small prayer rooms, which are known in Islam by their technical names such as *hawazas*, *Musaliyas*, *zawiyas*, etc. To understand the place of a mosque and its importance please refer to the book: *The Mosque Exposed* by these authors.

2. **To Listen:** Listening is to submit to the authority of the Qur'an and the *Sunnah*, i.e. The example of Muhammad[5].

3. **To Obey:** The obedience unto Allah through those in authority over the community is a Qur'anic injunction[6]. Sura 4:59 states:

> "O you who believe! Obey Allah and obey the Messenger, and those of you who are in authority."

Those in authority, means the Imams and the Islamic scholars, i.e. the so-called *Ulama*.

4. **To Immigrate:** Those verses have been mentioned above 2:218; 8:72,74,75;9:30,16:41;16:110; conjoining 'belief' with 'Immigration.'

5. **To Wage Jihad:** *Jihad* being here a commandment and duty imposed on all able Muslims. This duty is mostly seen by non-Muslims as self-sacrifice like that of suicidal missions. But from the Qur'anic prospective it could be anything from sacrifice of one's comfort by immigration, to spending or supporting with one's finances, or any other kind of facilitation for those involved in *jihad*. Just as fasting and prayer are obligatory duties so is *jihad*. We will but quote one reference here, Sura 2:216:

> "*Jihad* (holy fighting in Allah's Cause) is ordained for you (Muslims) though you dislike it, and it may be that you dislike a thing which is good for you and that you like a thing which is bad for you. Allah knows but you do not know."

In equating *jihad* with immigration, it makes immigration a stepping stone for greater goals, particularly of transforming the existing community into an Islamic one. Transforming an existing community means having it Islamised. This could be

---

[5] See the section "Example of the Prophet" P20
[6] ibid

achieved by a slow drip, drip effect with a constant demand(s) or negative comment(s) on the standard of the community; by being vocal and making demands for the integrity and rights of the Muslim community; by conditioning the host community to the supremacy of Islam; by intermarriage (These of course would only be Muslim men marrying local girls from the host society, and not allowing Muslim girls to marry non-Muslim men unless they convert to Islam). By these directives and actions, the society is ultimately transformed thus making Islam supreme and superior to all other systems especially in the socio-political sphere of that community.

It has been reported that Muhammad stated, "Migration cannot be ended as long as there is *kufr* (unbelief) or as long as there is an enemy that resists"[7], (*kenz al Umal* 46274). In other words, as long as there are communities out there that are non-Muslim, where Islam is not regarded as a supreme system, then *jihad* must continue. *Jihad* may be manifested in various forms but all of it would have one aim and that is to establish the supremacy of Islam. Hence Muhammad made it clear that migration is a duty that needs to be upheld forever or until the earth has submitted to the Islamic hegemony:

> "O people, immigrate, holding on to Islam, for *Hijra* (or migration) is to continue as long as *jihad* continues" (*kenz al Umal* 46260)[8].

In light of such subtle political doctrines being upheld and taught with religious vigour and zeal, one needs to consider the ever increasing Muslim immigration and their biological multiplication particularly in the West, and to other non-Muslim countries generally. In light of the foregoing one has to pose some important questions:

---

[7] http://www.al-eman.com/Islamlib/viewchp.asp?BID=137&CID=647&SW=46274#SR1

[8] ibid

1. Is it possible that we could see a day when the West would be transformed into a majority Muslim population as forecasted by demographical studies? And if so,

2. Would the Western world move into the fold of *Dar Al Islam* (the abode of Islam)?

3. Is it possible that as an abode of Islam the new West (that is Islamised Europe and USA) would be the one raising the banner of Allah holding his word uppermost, and its citizens conducting *jihad* for the sake of Allah, the very thing they fought so hard against?

MUSLIM IMMIGRATION OR ISLAMIC CONQUEST?

As stated earlier everyone knows that there are a variety of reasons and causes for everyday migration: economic, political, religious, social, natural disasters, wars, etc., but here we are only considering the migration of the Muslims to non-Islamic countries, prompted by religious edict, no matter how innocent and unconnected it may outwardly look at first.

It is important to understand that not all Muslim migrations to non-Muslim countries come under the religious banner — i.e. sanctioned by religious teaching — and remains political, despite all the exceptions. As will be explained, Muhammad's *Sunnah* contains all the needed directives to consolidate the Muslim immigrant community and to establish it as a dynamic and forward socio-political force, even when the original intent of the immigrants is to seek other goals, including the stray cases of those who aim at being integrated into the host society.

The Islamic community consolidation system works through a network of volunteers and other paid 'pious' individuals who act as community or mosque liaison officers, who keep a close eye on the community by policing the new immigrant arrivals. As the new migrants naturally gravitate to the food stores of their country of origin or other places of meeting such as cafes, restaurants, and other outlets, the community/mosque workers take it in turn to frequent these places and introduce themselves to the new migrants. These volunteers are very smooth and skillful salesmen who know how to express sympathy and empathy to the new migrants. They offer help and, knowing the systems of the host country, they quickly manage to facilitate a lot of things for the new migrants. They have access to a network of facilities from houses for temporary accommodation, to money to lend, to free food supply and other basic necessities which the migrant might need to settle. From here onwards it is a long road into drafting them into their ranks without the migrants knowledge, through a slow but steady programme of gradual indoctrination. The mosque/community workers cast their nets very wide, meaning that though they are always on the lookout for new arrivals, they do not limit their activities only towards them, they work even harder in recruiting new converts to Islam from the host community, as well as the children of the migrants who may be in their third or fourth generation. It is important to understand that none of those activities are limited to the disgruntled, but it is carried out across the board. The major aim is first and foremost to consolidate the existing Muslim community, and only in so doing successfully would it be possible to declare and fight for *Shariah* and the gaining of a special status for the Muslim community.

The first foundational principle for the creation of a successfully visible Islamic society is to be **separate** and **distinct**. The success is in segregation and this comes about through various steps prescribed by Islamic doctrines. So it is of absolute and paramount importance to grasp those Islamic terms, doctrines, rules and regulations under which much is licensed, and as such understand their implications from an Islamic jurisprudence point of view.

Directives that prohibit solitary immigration or immigration with a view to integration

Hadith number 2645 as reported by Abu Daw'uad[9], and the same reported by Tirmizi[10] in his manual *A-JJamieha* as *Hadith* number 1640, both quote Muhammad as saying:

> "I am innocent or free of every/any Muslim that lives amongst the Pagans/non-Muslims"

---

[9] http://www.qarn15.net/f/f1/f1f5/f1f5f18.htm

[10] http://www.qarn15.net/f/f1/f1f5/f1f5f19.htm

meaning that he — Muhammad — would not respond to them, neither will he intercede for them, nor implore Allah for his forgiveness for them. Also that he (Muhammad) is absolved of his responsibilities towards them as they had committed *kufr* (disbelief and betrayal) by associating with the non-Muslims, even if they be the host community.

By so doing, Muhammad forbade his followers to travel or to immigrate to a non-Muslim country or to relate to a non-Muslim society if it were to be limited to only their own personal gain or pleasure. However, they were and are allowed both pleasure and personal gain should the ultimate aim of advancing the cause of Islam be in some way part of the reason for their migration — whether it be permanent or temporary. This was a cunning military strategy on Muhammad's part.

In other words: 'no integration' with the host society. Now if one's entry visa or livelihood is based on showing some kind of integration[11] in order that the 'enemy' (i.e. non-Muslim host society) is satisfied, then it must be in appearance only and temporary until the Islamisation objective is achieved. (See the section on *Mud'arat*)

Further, Abu Daw'uad reports in *Hadith* number 2789[12] that Muhammad had said "whosoever collegiates or aggregates with non-Muslims and lives with them, he is one of them." Meaning whoever does this would not be regarded as a Muslim and is liable of being declared a *Kafir (non-believer)*."

Al Hakim[13] rewords it saying, "Do not inhabit or settle with non–Muslims and do not collegiate with them, for whoever does is not one of us."

---

[11] http://www.islam-qa.com/en/ref/27211/???%20?????%20???%20

   & http://www.islam-qa.com/en/ref/13694/???%20?????%20???%20

[12] http://www.al-eman.com/Hadeeth/viewchp.asp?BID=7&CID=34&SW=2787#SR1

[13] States Al Mustarak vol 2 page 141

Segregation is a Qur'anic foundational doctrine, which comes as a part of *Al Wala' wa Al Bara'* (Allegiance and Rejection)[14]. Though it is deduced from numerous Qur'anic passages we will mention only two Qur'anic references:

> Sura 58:22 "You will not find any people who believe in Allah and the Last Day, making friendship with those who oppose Allah and His Messenger, even though they were their fathers, or their sons, or their brothers, or their kindred (people). For such He has written Faith in their hearts, and strengthened them with the spirit from Himself. And We will admit them to Gardens (Paradise) under which rivers flow, to dwell therein (forever). Allah is pleased with them, and they with Him. They are the Party of Allah. Verily, it is the Party of Allah that will be the successful."

> Sura 9:29 "Fight against those who (1) believe not in Allah, (2) nor in the Last Day, (3) nor forbid that which has been forbidden by Allah and His Messenger (4) and those who acknowledge not the religion of truth (i.e. Islam) among the people of the Scripture (Jews and Christians), until they pay the *Jizyah* with willing submission, and feel themselves subdued."

This demand of segregation was established as described above, through Qur'anic doctrines and the *Sunnah*. As to the example of Muhammad who added to the *Hadith* references previously noted, we add one further tradition reported by Imam Abu Hanifa, the *Hadith* scholar and A'Nissai:

> Imam Ahmed Abu Hanifa[15] and A'Nissai[16] report a man called Jarir who went to pledge his allegiance to the

---

[14] See elaboration on this doctrine in the authors' response to the "Common Word" controversy (http://pilcrowpress.com/response.php)

[15] Musand Ahmed vol 4 /365

[16] Sunnan A'Nissai 4177

prophet. Muhammad set the following conditions or terms before accepting Jarir's pledge of allegiance and support that "he (Jarir) would worship Allah, establish regular prayers, pay zakat, will be loyal to the Muslims, would discriminate against the non-Muslims and will segregate himself from the Pagans or polytheists."

The foregoing clearly shows that the rule is that if the Muslims choose to be domiciled in non-Muslim countries or societies then it must be their prime aim to establish themselves for the benefit of Islam. They must become a vocal community that would sway power, or a state within a state, which would be Islamic. If the above were not their primary objective, then it would be in their interest and religiously speaking, they would be under obligation to return or move back from their new environment of a non-Muslim country to a Muslim country.

However, the reality is that no matter how hard one may try, once he/she migrates, they have to deal with the non-Muslim state, laws, and legal system, which is regarded as an apostate system and deal with the non-Muslims, who are regarded as *kafirs* by Islam.

This has led many to ask:

1. *Why* are the Muslims migrating in their masses to the West and multiplying?

2. *How* is it possible for the Muslims to justify their existence in the West despite those directives?

3. Is it possible that Muslims are migrating in defiance of Islam or is it somehow justified, and if justified then how and under what injunctions?

Not being aware of various intricate Islamic doctrines, it has been concluded by many of our Western experts that these migrations are mostly economic, and they have failed to identify the doctrines behind the 'how' questions, too.

Surprisingly the 'why' question (No. 1 above) has been clarified by many *fatwas*[17] that have been, and continue to be, issued by Muslim scholars, requiring those Muslims, who are immigrating to non-Muslim countries, especially to the West, to spread and establish Islam as a religion as well as a political and governing system. In fact the subject matter of this book is to qualify this very statement. The serious reader is asked to review Appendix A to obtain the full logic based on Islamic jurisprudence and from well-recognised Islamic authorities.

As to the second issue of the 'how' questions (No. 2 and 3 above), i.e. how do Muslims manage to make the forbidden lawful in order to be able to live in the West, is strategically more important and will be handled first.

From an Islamic point of view the answer as to how the forbidden or the *haram* has been moved or changed into the realm of *halal* or allowed and sanctioned, is rooted in two Islamic disciplines:

(a) Religious doctrinal injunctions, and

(b) Islamic jurisprudence directives.

Both the religious doctrinal injunctions and the jurisprudence directives are interwoven, so it is the Islamic jurisprudence directive which is followed, but it is those very directives that the Jurists issue, are based on, or are deduced from the religious doctrines. These religious doctrines are in turn authentic and valid because of the sources from which they are drawn from.

These religious doctrines are drawn from two sources, both of which are regarded as primary sources; these being the Qur'an and the *Sunnah* (or the example of the prophet).

---

[17] See Appendix A

UNDERSTANDING THE FORMATION OF JURISTIC DIRECTIVES

Juristic directives are naturally issued by Muslim scholars, on the authoritative teachings of the Qur'an and the *Sunnah* — that is the example of Muhammad — his deeds, words or to what he consented. Appropriately using the two together formulates concepts or doctrines.

These concepts and doctrines in turn have been formulated into categories or situations that explain and stipulate what is allowed under what conditions, when and to whom!

So let's turn to our question of: *How does the forbidden get transformed into the permitted?*

Facilitation through tay'seer

The starting point for new immigrants and converts to Islam is to facilitate their transition through some easy terms. Whatever Islam commands them to do is done in such a way as to make their burdens initially light. Muhammad achieved this by establishing a concept or category known as *tay'asur* or *tay'seer* meaning 'making it easy, facilitating' or 'lightening one's burden', based on the following sections of the Qur'anic verses (marked in different font):

> Sura 2:185 "The month of Ramadan in which was revealed the Qur'an, a guidance for mankind and clear proofs for the guidance and the criterion (between right and wrong). So whoever of you sights (the crescent on

the first night of) the month (of Ramadan i.e. is present at his home), he must observe *Saum* (fasts) that month, and whoever is ill or on a journey, the same number [of days which one did not observe *Saum* (fasts) must be made up] from other days. **Allah intends for you ease, and He does not want to make things difficult for you.** (He wants that you) must complete the same number (of days), and that you must magnify Allah for having guided you so that you may be grateful to Him."

Sura 4:28 "**Allah wishes to lighten (the burden) for you:** and man was created weak."

Sura 2:286 "**Allah burdens not a person beyond his scope.** He gets reward for that (good) which he has earned, and he is punished for that (evil) which he has earned. "Our Lord! Punish us not if we forget or fall into error, our Lord! Lay not on us a burden like that which You did lay on those before us (Jews and Christians); **our Lord! Put not on us a burden greater than we have strength to bear.** Pardon us and grant us Forgiveness. Have mercy on us. You are our *Maulana* (Patron, Supporter and Protector, etc.) and give us victory over the disbelieving people."

Sura 65:7 "Let the rich man spend according to his means, and the man whose resources are restricted, let him spend according to what Allah has given him. **Allah puts no burden on any person beyond what He has given him.** Allah will grant after hardship, ease."

In other words, it's clear from the above verses that it is the desire and the will of Allah to lighten the burden on the Muslims in every aspect whether it be religious, economical, social, etc. But that does not mean total suspension of the duties for everyone. So the category is limited to those who cannot bear the burden, or who have limited resources, or are weak, etc., or to those who need the injunctions to overcome the hardships. Though outwardly they may seem to be disobeying, inwardly it would have been done to achieve that which is required of them, whatever the case may be.

In other words, they have a need. This 'need' is now another category. This 'need' may be a zeal to spread Islam but they are really unable to do so due to their personal weakness in the sense that there might be many temptations for them to compromise with the enemy. The enemy's lifestyle may look so attractive, etc., or on the other hand it may not be a personal weakness but an enforced situation of compulsion. This compulsion may mean walking contrary to Islamic teaching such as working in a mixed environment of men and women, or serving or handling forbidden products such as swine or alcohol, etc. In other words, something that may be enforced against the will of the one concerned. It may be unseen circumstances, tangible difficulties, or just perceived ones. Whatever the factors may be, this has been identified by the Qur'anic injunctions as *darura'* (or necessity).

Darura' or necessity

These so-called 'necessities or compulsions' are governed by further sub-categories and directives based on how Muhammad dealt with his own necessities, thus completing the Qur'anic revelations throughout his life.

Here are some of the *darura'* verses;

> Sura 6:119 "And why should you not eat of that (meat) on which Allah's Name has been pronounced (at the time of slaughtering the animal), while He has explained to you in detail what is forbidden to you, except under compulsion of necessity? And surely many do lead (mankind) astray by their own desires through lack of knowledge. Certainly your Lord knows best the transgressors."
>
> Sura 5:3 "Forbidden to you (for food) are: the dead animals – (cattle-beast not slaughtered), blood, the flesh of swine, and the meat of that which has been slaughtered as a sacri-

fice for others than Allah, or has been slaughtered for idols, etc., or on which Allah's Name has not been mentioned while slaughtering, and that which has been killed by strangling, or by a violent blow, or by a headlong fall, or by the goring of horns — and that which has been (partly) eaten by a wild animal — unless you are able to slaughter it (before its death) — and that which is sacrificed (slaughtered) on An-Nusub (stone altars). (Forbidden) also is to use arrows for seeking luck or decision, (all) that is Fisqun (disobedience of Allah and sin). This day, those who disbelieved have given up all hope of your religion, so fear them not, but fear Me. This day, I have perfected your religion for you, completed My Favour upon you, and have chosen for you Islam as your religion. But as for him who is forced by severe hunger, with no inclination to sin (such can eat these above-mentioned meats), then surely, Allah is Oft-Forgiving, Most Merciful."

So under the *darura'* (necessities), the forbidden becomes lawful, the exception becomes the rule, and the rule as we know it is suspended until the circumstances change or the objectives are achieved. Hence this principle is applied to overcome every obstacle by Muslims in a non-Muslim country from visa regulations, to obtaining nationality of the host country, to ushering in Islamic *Shariah* slowly (take for instance all these years when the Muslims who worked in supermarkets in UK handling pork and alcohol, because they were weak, the *darura'* concept kicked in, however, when the Muslim community grew in numbers and strength, they are able to voice objections and manage to obtain favourable results from their employers).

The *darura'* permits addressing the Muslim community demands as though these were requests that can be changed subject to the views of those in power. But ultimately these demands get achieved using existing loopholes in the laws. This is done through various means but most of the time by setting a precedent, in that those things would be implemented in the closed Muslim society in a number of districts or provinces/counties of the host country. Naturally they are backed by their mosques and other recognised Islamic outfits, which are on good terms with the government and always giving the impression that they are most moderate and are most law abiding people. They are, however, simultaneously working through a network of people and institutions who oversee a concerted programme of a 'total change' of the host society.

As stated before, all these demands come in as requests and legitimate religious rights that are usually voiced by converts from the host society who are articulate and well-received. Those demands come in sporadically, here and there on different issues, mostly viewed as insignificant by the host society. Yet these demands have the inbuilt potential of undoing the whole system and ultimately ushering in the *Shariah* (Islamic law) step by step.

Meanwhile the host society is helplessly watching the rise of the Islamic practices and emerging lifestyles as new phenomena, with varying reactions from utter horror, to being conditioned to accepting it, to an attitude of a new normality, to adopting it and ultimately becoming part of it.

For example, consider the simple issue of the Islamic dress code. Some think that it may be cultural while others regard it as religious. In either case, it demotes women and treats them as unequal, mentally deformed and something that must not be in the public eye. The dress code brings in the whole concept of a segregated society within the Muslim set up. In time, once accepted, the segregated society and all its directives will usher in Islamic regulations.

Once the host society accepts the segregated Muslim society, demands are made for separate swimming pools or times when no males can be admitted. Once achieved, demands would move to schools and other public areas. Demands are made that no male doctor, Muslim or non-Muslim, has the right to examine a Muslim woman, so hospitals and clinics are forced to provide female doctors. With this directive, there are some strong objections expressed, but they will go unnoticed. Meanwhile the whole community will not realise that *Shariah* is being ushered in right under their noses. This is only one example as to how the Islamic agenda is propelled from every direction.

Sheikh Baz[18] who used to be the chairman of all *Ulama* in Saudi Arabia, and a leading Saudi Scholar, was asked, "What is the Islamic view if one were to travel to the country of pagans accompanied by one's wife?" His response[19] was that it is forbidden to travel to a land of the pagans and to be a resident there, but an exception is made that for those who are knowledgeable in their religion and are able to spread Islam, able to guard themselves, and are unlikely to fall in the snares of the pagans. Then there would be no objections to them going there, and none of the restrictions would be applicable.

Saleh Al Fawazan, another very well known scholar and jurist, added[20] that besides preaching Islam, other aims must be to strengthen the existing Muslim communities in the land of the unbelievers, and if none of these are the among the aims of the immigrant then he will have committed a sin by migrating.

---

[18] Sheikh Abdel Aziz Bin Abdullah bin Baz, a very famous Saudi Islamic scholar born in 1910 and who at the age of 27 was appointed to the Judiciary, holding various positions. He was the Chair the of senior clerics in Saudi Arabia, the head of the research and fatwa dept, founder and chair of the Islamic world league, head of the world council of mosques, author of many books, articles, and issued hundreds of fatwa. He died in 2000.

[19] http://www.sobe3.com/vb/showthread.php?t=4128

[20] ibid

REASONS FOR AND GOALS OF THE LEGITIMATE ISLAMIC MIGRATIONS

He is mistaken who thinks that the Islamic conquest that was started by Muhammad some 1400 years ago is over. The conquest that Muhammad started is still continuing from Moscow to New York and from Barcelona to Brazil. Whosoever regards that the *Hijra*, or the migration, was once from Mecca to Medina some 1400 years ago is also wrong Islamically speaking. For Muhammad said that:

> "Migration will continue until the sun rises from the West. *Hijra* would not be stopped until repentance is cut off, and repentance will not be cut off until the sun rises from the West."
>
> Reported by Ahmed and Abu Daw'uad *Hadith* No 3453.

Hijra (migration) ceases only when a place, a community or a country has been won over, or as per Islamic terminology, the *fateh* (conquest) has been achieved. Only then, there is no *Hijra* as stated in *Hadith* number 3455. In other words, though the Muslim migrants may continue their movement, it would be regarded as an internal move from one location already to another because that state or location would have been classified or identified as an Islamic territory. A given location might be only a district of a city — like Mississauga in Toronto, Canada or Dewsbury in Yorkshire, England — that may have been taken over by a large Muslim population. The Muslims would be running various Islamic institutions and generally having an upper hand with a considerable disregard to the laws of the land. As such, the cities would be subjected to the Islamic way of life with *Shariah* as the form of its governance. Therefore, so-called newcomers or immigrants would not be entitled to the extraordinary conditions and stipulations that were the privilege of those early pioneers who came while the location was *dar al kufr* or the abode of unbelief.

However, the newcomer's reward would be greater than that of the pioneers as their responsibilities would be graver. As stated before, Muhammad said that:

> "There can be no *Hijra*, (migration) after the conquest but *jihad* and a desire or an intention, and if you settle then spread out." (Reported by Bukhari)

In other words, though a Muslim community would have been established with mosques and other Islamic institutions with a say, its sphere of influence would be very limited and could be surrounded by *kufr* (unbelief). Thus it would be the task of the newcomers or the new generation, i.e., the offspring of the earlier pioneers, to see that *jihad* is waged for the sake of Allah and Islam is feared and given the honour due to it.

So then their newly settled community may be in their third or fourth generation as immigrants, who officially may not be regarded as immigrants, take upon themselves the desire, the intention to wage *jihad* for the sake of Allah and take Islam even further (as one sees in UK, and elsewhere in Europe). The real threat of terrorism would be coming from these very quarters. The concept of intention for *jihad* and the taking of more territory has been expounded and explained much more by Sheik A'zammal in his book: *Jihad and the intention for it*, the text of which is available on the internet[21].

Let us now turn back to *Hijra*, or specifically Muslim migrations, as their nature is distinct from all other kinds of migrations. For *Hijra* as an Islamic concept doesn't mean only change of one's living location

---

[21] Sheik Abdel Muhssen bin Abdullah A'zamaal
   http://www.taimiah.org/Display.asp?ID=94&t=book80&pid=2&f=bmr00081.htm

or residency from one country to another, but the whole transformation of understanding, customs, behaviour, rules and regulations through the political power base to a pro-Islamic one, if not outrightly Islamic. Thus, it is a movement from the state of freedom to enslavement to Allah, as the Islamic expression goes.

THE GOAL OF MIGRATION

Having dealt with the 'how', that is to say the question of justification or of 'easing the burden', and *darura*' (necessity) that prompts the application of extraordinary rules, and suspending all the norms, we now turn our attention to the aims, objectives, and goals of the Islamic migration and the appropriate directives by which these objectives and goals are governed.

The **primary** goal of the *Hijra* (Islamic immigration) is the establishment of an Islamic state. This is achieved through *da'wa*. *Da'wa* means 'to call', and in Islamic terms it means 'a call to Islam' and so it is a missionary call to embrace Islam. It is unlike a personal conversion call, though at the outset it may look like that. *Da'wa* is both religious and political as there is no separation between sacred and secular, between state and religion in Islam. The *da'wa* is to spread the message of Islam and the establishment of an Islamic state. The spreading of Islam is not simply a missionary activity like that of a church but it is the establishment of a community that would rise up as the soldiers of Allah to establish an Islamic state. The Islamic confession and its declaration ultimately state that the suzerainty of this world and all its governments belongs to Allah and his messenger Muhammad. Therefore, it is Allah and his apostle who are the only rightful legislators. All other legislations are manmade, and as such they are to be disregarded as *kufr*, or unbelief and apostasy (more on this under *tamkeen*). Because of this, the primary goal of the Islamic migration or *Hijra* is considered to be, by Muslim scholars from a religious and jurisprudence point of view as the vanguard, a preamble and prelude to *jihad*, for the establishment of an Islamic state.

It is clearly stated by Sheikh Mansour[22], who says that Qur'anically speaking *Hijra* is always preceded by faith, and followed by *jihad* in the cause of Allah. In other words the migration itself is faith and the practical outcome of the *Hijra* is *jihad* for the sake of Allah.

Mansour and the other Muslim scholars have based their deliberations on the following Qur'anic verses:

> 2:218 "Verily, those who have believed, and those who have emigrated (for Allah's Religion) and have striven hard in the Way of Allah, or (fought Jihad for the sake of Allah) all these hope for Allah's Mercy. And Allah is Oft-Forgiving, Most-Merciful."
>
> 8:72 "Verily, those who believed, and emigrated and strove hard and fought with their property and their lives in the Cause of Allah."
>
> 8:74 "And those who believed, and emigrated and strove hard in the Cause of Allah (Al-Jihad)."
>
> 9:20 "Those who believed (in the Oneness of Allah — Islamic Monotheism) and emigrated and strove hard and fought in Allah's Cause with their wealth and their lives are far higher in degree with Allah. They are the successful ones."

Sheikh Halima[23] states that among the aims and the objectives of the *Hijra* migration are:

1. To revive *jihad*,

2. To strengthen the Muslims, and

3. To establish their authority over the non-Muslims.

---

[22] Sheikh Dr. Muhammad Mutawali Mansour a professor at Al-Azhar University, an author of many Islamic books, extremely popular as a presenter and producer of many Islamic TV programs. http://www.islamonline.net/arabic/Daawa/2006/02/article01.shtml

[23] Well known by his nick name Abu Baseer aTarsusi, extremely popular left his home land of Syria for the sake of his religion

For *Hijra* and *jihad* are inseparable companions. Each component (that is *Hijra* and *jihad*) is needed for the survival of the other. All this has been clearly demonstrated by the Qur'anic verses quoted above. He goes on to say:

> "There can be no empowerment of religion without *Hijra* or immigration, neither can Islam be demonstrated in the abode of unbelief, if the Muslims were not to immigrate and settle there, nor would the power of Islam be felt if the Muslims were to remain a few, without the increase in their numbers nor without the help of the arrivals of new and more Muslims." (http://www.saaid.net/Doat/Zugail/166.htm)

Sheikh Muhammad Abdel Wahab[24], the founder of Wahabism, states in his book on *jihad*[25] that *Hijra* is a must for those who are able to display and practice their religion openly, for they will be able to perform *jihad* and would be multiplying the numbers of Muslims.

Sheikh Hussein Shahata[26], a well-known Islamic thinker, says that the *Hijra* from Mecca to Medina was for the sake of the religion of Allah and the establishment of an Islamic state, and to spread it all over the world as an example and a model. The *Hijra* from Mecca to Medina is considered to be a *jihad* for the sake of religion. In other words, the *Hijra* of Muhammad was not just a human activity but it was ordained; and he did it for the sake of establishing the religion of Allah. For with the *Hijra* came the establishment of the new Muslim community and with the community came the need for new legislation, then the ushering in of an Islamic state, followed by the principles of war and peace, courts,

---

[24] Founder of Wahabi school, deeply influenced by Ibn Taymiyya

[25] http://www.kl28.com/books/showbook.php?bID=37&pNo=1

[26] http://www.ikhwanonline.com/Article.asp?ArtID=33506&SecID=363 Dr Shahat holds a PhD in the philosophy of management accounts from Bradford University UK, an authority on Islamic finances, *zakat* and other matters, an Islamic thinker and writer on various Islamic issues.

taxation, and treaties with the non-Muslims, the conduct of Muslims and the legislation of how to run their daily lives.

Dr Salah a'din Sultan[27], a professor of Islamic jurisprudence at Cairo University and the head of the American Islamic University, states that the settlement of some Muslims in the West is an absolute must, forming and reorganising the Muslim community as a new force to proclaim the message of Islam. As seen earlier, 'proclaiming the message of Islam' is a technical term that is all-encompassing, which in simple language means to establish an Islamic community that in due time will be ushering in and enforcing the *Shariah* as a way of life.

Based on all the foregoing, from the Islamic jurisprudence view the immigration of the Muslims to the West is to be regarded as the most important step on the ladder for achieving the establishment of an Islamic state in the West. This is the primary objective of Islamic mission in the West.

This is what Sheikh Abdel Khaliq[28] states in his book, *The Primaries of the Islamic Mission to the West*[29]. Among many other things, he suggests the consolidation of the Muslim communities and their loyalties and allegiance to the international Islamic *Ummah*, and not to the system of unbelief where that community finds itself; meaning neither accommodating the host society nor consenting to any of its values.

In his opinion, the Muslim community must be well-versed in their religion, particularly the Islamic doctrine of *tawheed*, which is

---

[27] A famous Egyptian born Muslim preacher resident of Bahrain, holds a professorship at many Universities, Bahrain, Cairo, Columbus Ohio, Michigan, open American University, Boston, author of many books, articles and regular commentator on Islamic matters, has issued numerous *fatawas*
http://www.islamonline.net/Arabic/Daawa/2003/08/article09.shtml

[28] Sheikh Dr. Abdel Rahman bin Abdel Khaliq born in Egypt in 1939, professor of Islamic shar'iah, has authored many books especially on loyalty and allegiance of Muslims

[29] http://www.islamonline.net/arabic/daawa/2002/07/article06.shtml & http://www.salafi.net/books/book29.html

absolute monotheism. They must go ahead with the establishment of mosques everywhere — staffed with sound Imams. He puts a lot of emphasis on public prayers to be conducted regularly as a visible display of the Islamic community and its presence. They must also hire preachers, establish libraries, research centres, facilities for children, classes and special days for locals and inquirers, thus making inroads into the host communities.

The learning of Arabic must be given top priority. Khaliq goes on to emphasise that the children of the immigrants must be taught Arabic not only so that they pray, but much more, to be articulate in the language. This will keep them rooted in the homelands of their parents and grandparents.

He continues by quoting the *fatwa* of Sheikh Abu Bakr Jabir Al Jazeeri that high on the agenda of the Muslim community must be to seek to obtain the nationality of the host country, and among other priorities, to stand for local and national elections, to defend the causes of the Muslim community. He concludes that the immigration of the Muslims to non-Muslim countries and especially to the West is to empower and consolidate Islam as a preamble to *jihad*. All of this is legally binding on all Muslims.

THE 'WHAT' COMPONENTS
OF THE HIJRA

A quick review

So far, we have explained the 'how,' i.e. transforming the *haram* (forbidden) into the *halal* (allowed and sanctioned), and the aims and the goals of the *Hijra* as being paired with *jihad* to Islamise the host community.

We introduced some of the roots of *Hijra* in the life of Muhammad and its various injunctions in the Qur'an. We have also considered 'the five charges', which correspond to the outworking of the *jihad* from within through various Islamic principles of 'lightening the burdens' (*tayseer*) by suspending the Qur'anic rules as seen per necessity (*darura'*).

We also demonstrated that *Hijra* in Islam has aims, objectives, and purposes. These are operated under conditions and tactics considered of divine origin as they stem from the Qur'an and the *Sunnah*.

Now we turn to a very important component of the movement itself. We turn our attention to the principles, purposes and the programs of 'what' is to be done to integrate the newcomers into the existing Muslim society in foreign countries (or non-Islamic lands) yet segregating themselves from the host society in that very society — to achieve the aims and the goals of the immigration as being the Islamisation of the host society and the establishment of an Islamic state.

According to the Islamic jurisprudence there are two most important tasks to be undertaken; these being **tamkeen** and **i'dad**. Even before we introduce and explain these terms, it is worthwhile noting that these two are inseparable, like a bank or currency note with different images on each side that are inseparable, thus making it valid legal tender, yet one note. Hence it will not be easy to separate them and explain each fully on its own, as these are deeply interlinked, and one without the other does not function nor can it exist.

Tamkeen or empowerment

Tamkeen means to strengthen, to deepen, to intensify, to enable, to consolidate or to empower.

In other words, this occurs through the deepening of convictions of the existing Muslim community, be it the first generation of immigrants or fourth generation who may be born and bred in that community, as well as the new immigrants. Having deepened and intensified their convictions would lead to a consolidation of their Islamic identity through which their voice will be strengthened above all other voices, demanding to be governed, and to be able to run their lives in accordance with the Islamic Law; this is *Shariah*. In Islamic terms, *tamkeen* means to rule in a matter or to have total control in a given matter.

I'dad or preparation

I'dad, or preparation, has a dual concept of readying, drawing up, setting up; and that of increase or multiplication of numbers. So it means 'to be prepared and ready.' Qur'anically speaking it means to be ready and prepared with military equipment that would be a force, for without such preparation *tamkeen* has neither value nor can violent *jihad* be waged.

Unlike *tamkeen* which is more personal, *i'dad* is more structural and communal. It is the preparation of arms, and command control centres, the formation of systems, impartation of skills, and formulating co-ordinated efforts across various networks to enable the launching of *jihad* when and if necessary.

Of course, there is much more to both concepts of *tamkeen* and *i'dad*, but many of their details — that run into a number of sections and sub-sections — are not directly relevant to our topic so we will only explore that which is most relevant to our subject matter. For instance, there is an ideological *i'dad*, or preparation, as well as a practical *i'dad*. Practical *i'dad* is necessary training and preparation that would facilitate a certain aspect of a given operation.

Two important forms of *tamkeen* (empowerment)

The tactical mechanisms of *tamkeen* are many. Here we will focus on two forms:

1. Internal *tamkeen* or consolidation within the Muslim community, and

2. External *tamkeen* with both Muslims and non-Muslims.

First the internal consolidation: Islamically speaking, the strengthening process is the most important process, although it is slow and most time-consuming. But it remains the one that occupies the Muslims and their leaders the most.

Getting deeper in Islam is doctrinal and an integral part of consolidating one's religious beliefs and practices. In other words, this process can be best described as 'puritanical indoctrination.' In the beginning this is done very quietly and discreetly, if not secretly.

This is the first step in the establishment or consolidation of what one already has access to without raising an alarm. The infrastructures of *tamkeen* are in almost every Islamic outlet, from mosques to *madrassas*, Islamic cultural centres, Islamic schools, Muslim youth clubs, Muslim *da'wa* or mission centres, and all forms of Muslim mass media, etc.

The aim is consolidation of the members of the existing Muslim community and making them identifiably Muslims who would proudly defend their Islamic identity.

The term *tamkeen* itself is extracted from the Qur'an and translated in English as 'being established' or 'to establish':

Sura 18:84 "Surely We **established** him in the land and granted him means of access to everything."

Sura 7:10 "And certainly We have **established** you in the earth and made in it means of livelihood ."

Sura 12:56 "Thus did We give **established** power to Joseph in the land, to take possession therein as, when, or where he pleased. We bestow of our Mercy on whom We please, and We suffer not, to be lost, the reward of those who do good."

Sura 28:6 "And to **establish** them in the land, and We let Pharaoh and Haman and their hosts receive from them that which they feared."

Sura 22:41 "Those who, should We **establish** them in the land, will keep up prayer and pay the poor-rate and enjoin good and forbid evil; and Allah's is the end of affairs."

Notable Islamic scholars such as A'Salabi[30] and Al Shaheri[31] have written extensively on this topic.

Of course, *Hijra* (immigration) is the first step towards *tamkeen*, establishment and consolidation in non-Muslim lands. Citing the example of Ibrahim (Abraham) who immigrated:

Sura 29:26 "So Lout (Lot) believed in him (Abraham's Message). He (Abraham)] said: 'I will emigrate for the sake of my Lord. Verily, He is the All-Mighty, the All-Wise.'"

The *Hijra* was one of the most important factors in the process of consolidation and empowerment of Muhammad when he and his followers immigrated to Medina.

---

[30] http://www.islamtoday.net/articles/show_articles_content.cfm?id=177&catid=191&artid=7135 born in Libya obtained his doctorate in tamkeen Islamic Jurisprudence from Umm Durman Islamic University in 1999 author of various books on tamkeen and sira of the companions

[31] http://mahawer.al-islam.com/dawaBooks/078.doc

Al Shaharie expounds this in his book (عوامـل النصـر والتمكيــن في دعــوات المرســلين) *Factors of Victory in the Establishment (Tamkeen) of Calls of the Messengers.*

In other words, the doctrinal preparation of the inner commitment and the impartation of the convictions that the host community is evil and anti-Islamic would lead to and necessitate the establishment of a separate and segregated Muslim community that would be charged to purge the evil from the host society.

As soldiers of Allah, it would be the duty of these Muslims to see that the enemies of Allah are eliminated or subjugated. This would be done in stages starting with those in the immediate vicinity who might be most outspoken against Islam and its 'barbaric' system. The immediate vicinity obligates the local cell or active Islamic group to take responsibility for seeing that the enemies of Islam are dealt with appropriately, as per Sura 9:123,

> "O you who believe! Fight those of the disbelievers who are close to you, and let them find harshness in you, and know that Allah is with those who are the pious."

Those must be eliminated and it would be the duty of the faithful soldiers of Allah to purge the earth from the enemies of Allah who are nothing but corrupters. So clearly, once that doctrinal embellishment is achieved, then the physically violent *jihad* is a foregone conclusion. Sooner or later given the right cells and coordination, it will take place.

This concept of establishment or empowerment through *Hijra* or immigration is not just an emulation of a human being, namely Muhammad as a Prophet, but it is a command of Allah promising the Muslims victory and their establishment on earth as per Sura 24:55,

> "Allah has promised those among you who believe, and do righteous good deeds, that He will certainly grant them succession to (the present rulers) in the earth, as He granted it to those before them, and that He will grant them the authority to practice their religion, that

which He has chosen for them (i.e. Islam). And He will surely give them in exchange a safe security after their fear (provided) they (believers) worship Me and do not associate anything (in worship) with Me. But whoever disbelieved after this, they are the rebellious, disobedient to Allah."

It is important to understand the concept of doing 'good' by those who believe. That 'good' is not just helping the poor and the needy. It is much more. The pinnacle of that 'good' is to advance the religion of Allah, which has now been chosen for them, for it is his own religion as per Sura 3:19, "The religion before Allah is Islam" and no other religion or system is acceptable to Allah neither will he receive them here on earth nor the life after as stated in Sura 3:85,

"And whoever seeks a religion other than Islam, it will never be accepted of him, and in the Hereafter he will be one of the losers."

The advancement of the religion of Allah is a Muslim's duty. In this case, it is the duty of all Muslim believers to see the establishment of this religion; be they immigrants or residents, be they new arrivals or now in their fourth generation, be they from a different racial and ethnic background than those among whom they live, or be they the new converts of the indigenous people.

The external *takmeen* or consolidation of Islam with the Muslims and non-Muslims

This form of *tamkeen* is one of the most dangerous tactical mechanisms when used across the board with non-Muslims. This principle is called *Ta'leef al Qulub* or 'reconciliation of hearts'. In other words, it is a purposed plan to win a favourable position with the non-Muslims, making them favourably disposed towards Islam and Muslims. This is a Qur'anic doctrine, which was practiced by Muhammad, his companions, and continues to be practiced as we write. It occurs in Sura 9:60,

"*Zakat* are only for the poor, and those employed to collect (the funds); and to attract the hearts of those who have been inclined towards Islam; and to free the captives; and for those in debt; and for Allah's Cause (i.e. for *Mujahideen* — those fighting in the holy wars), and for the wayfarer; a duty imposed by Allah. And Allah is All-Knower, All-Wise."

Tabarie explains this verse by stating that as a newly converted Muslim accepts the prophet of Allah, he or she would be granted large portions from the *sadakat*, which is a religious tax. Accordingly, 'this is a good religious practice.'

The details of the legitimacy of this principle to sweeten the hearts of the enemies of Islam through payments either in cash or in kind can be found in all Islamic jurisprudence manuals[32] without exception.

Dr Ghazee Anayat[33], a leading jurist on *zakat* issues, states that 'reconciling hearts' is a form of *da'wa* to draw people to Islam. Ghazi is supported in his views by many Muslim scholars who say that this practice of 'reconciling hearts' cannot be redundant with the spread of Islam, but is needed as a firm factor in winning over the non-Muslims[34].

Hence, the reconciliation of hearts is an Islamic principle which grants the legitimacy to infiltrate all kinds of institutions in every field such as educational, health and welfare, security, mass media, economical and political in order to 'win over' individuals.

---

[32] Al Ahkam al Sultaniya al Marudi page 123; Al Ahkam al Sultaniya Al fura'a page 132; Rawdanat A'Talibeen Al Nawawi vol 2 page 313; A'Tasheel Ibn Jawziya Al Gharaneety vol 2 page 78 ; Tafseer Ibn Kathir vol 2 page 365; Fiqh al zakat Al Qardawi vol 2 page 603; Muqawimat al Iqtisad Al Islami Abed alSamie Al Masri 140; Tafseer Al Munir vol 10 page 270; Tafseer Al Tabari vol 4 page 313; Fath al Qadeer Al shawkani vol 2 page 374; Al Zakat fi Al Masaleeh al a'ama Dr Farees page 31; Al Zakat Al Jamamei page 72

[33] Istekhdam al wazafee Li al zakat Dr Ghazee Anayat page 48, 68-69

[34] http://web.macam.ac.il/~tawfieq/moallafa-2.htm

Dr Anayat states clearly in his book[35] that the purpose of payments to non-Muslims from the Islamic *zakat* is based on the principle of 'reconciling hearts'. It is to silence the critical voices of all non-Muslims and their objecting pens, which present Islam in a poor or bad light. And, by so doing, it is transforming those very voices and pens to becoming vocal for the cause of Islam. This, he suggests, must continue by gaining more and more media attention. In sum, they are seeking journalists to report on Islam in a kind-hearted manner.

The same tactic is articulated by Sheikh Dr. Mustapha Al-Zarka[36]. He writes that from one era to another the recipients would differ from paying tribal leaders in the past to newspaper owners in the present, or establishing new publications of glossy magazines or creating special media to promote Islam. Sheikh Saeed Al-Hawee[37] is also in agreement with Dr. Zarka on advancing a media campaign toward Islam.

While Dr. Abu Farees[38] says that the arrow of reconciling-the-hearts principle is one of the eternal miracles of the Islamic *Shariah*, it therefore must be used and implemented in its fullness. Saeed Al Hawee[39] furthers the point by saying that politicians are to be favoured. In other words, politicians must be recipients of such favours so that they will be well disposed towards Islam and Muslims.

Ibrahim Al-Qaptee, an Egyptian researcher, states that in the last few decades the social face of Europe has changed as the Muslim activists have continued their efforts to make Islam both a political and ideological force and a religion of the majority. This is not only through

---

[33] Istekhdam al wazafee Li al zakat Dr Ghazee Anayat page 48, 68-69

[34] http://web.macam.ac.il/~tawfieq/moallafa-2.htm

[35] Istekhdam al wazafee Li al zakat Dr Ghazee Anayat page 48, 68-69

[36] The late Dr Zarka was One of the most notable Hanbali Fiqh scholar of our time, Al Madkhal al Fiqhee al A'aam Mustapha Ahmed Al Zarka vol 1 page 160

[37] A prolific author of over 20 Shari'ah books, highly respected and popular among Shari'ah scholars. He was born in Syria and died in Jordan. Al Islam Saeed Al Hawee vol 1 page 124

[38] Infaq Al zakat fi al Masleeh al aa'ama Dr Abu Farees Page 35-36

[39] http://web.macam.ac.il/~tawfieq/moallafa-2.htm

the demographic increase but through infiltrating the social, civil, economical and political institutions of Europe. He goes on to state that this plan was published in the 1980s by the Islamic Council of Europe. This strategy is presented in a book called: *The Muslim Societies in non-Muslim Countries*. It instructs Muslims to live as segregated societies, ultimately requiring the Europeans to address and accommodate the social and religious needs of those communities. In so doing, Muslims are establishing clusters of Islamic societies fully equipped with religious and jurisprudence centres. They are avoiding integration with the European societies yet sustaining just enough contacts with non-Muslims for the propagation of Islam as a requirement on all Muslim believers in order to achieve the main objective of transforming the host societies into Islamic society where Islam would be supreme.

The same strategy was published by the Islamic foundation in the UK: *The Islamic Movement in the West* by the late Khuram Murad, being a blueprint of an Islamic takeover. One would ask how the moderates might view all this. Both sides agree fully with the final objective of the Islamisation of the West. The only difference was and continues to be in the methodology that would determine how fast or slow a Muslim should proceed with reconciliation of heart and whether a Muslim should resort to violent *jihad* or not, as to how effective it would be. But as we said before, both sides are in full agreement with the final objective of the Islamisation of the Western societies.

The implementation of this strategy is clear in what is happening in the UK, Sweden, Finland, Holland, France, Germany, Spain, Italy, Belgium, and Austria. It is so clearly shown by Shakeer A'Nabilisi's article on the Islamic infiltration of such prestigious American Universities as Harvard, the rest of the Ivy League[40] and others[41]. We can see the growth of mega-mosques financed by Saudi Arabia and UAE, the attack on the local churches and its ministers in so-called Islamic enclaves to purge those Islamic areas from non-Islamic influences. *Halal*

---

[40] http://www.alarabiya.net/views/2008/06/25/52060.html

[40] http://www.meforum.org/article/883

meat is already a reality in schools, prisons, hospitals, and public canteens in so many places — as is the *hijab*, public prayers, the massive financial investments[42], the implementation of the *Shariah*, and the official recognition by the British government of *Shariah* courts. All of these advances are mighty achievements of *tamkeen*. The favourable disposition of the mass media in the UK, especially the BBC as well as the US towards Islam, is due to the Islamic principle of *tamkeen*, which in turn is based in 'reconciling the hearts' methodology.

Strangely enough, Muslims are always levelling against the Christian the charge of 'buying' converts from Islam; yet nowhere in the New Testament can one find such doctrines.

I'dad (preparation or readying)

I'dad, or preparation, is linked and bound with equipment and specifically military equipment. But before we shed light on its Qur'anic roots, let us explain its place and importance in this empowerment process.

This readying process requires structures through which appropriate preparation can take place. Preparation can be from the simplest to the most complex. For instance, in simply knowing where Muslims are (surveillance), knowing what issues face them, and knowing how loyal they are to their Islamic commitments are all part of *i'dad*.

The readying process can occur in different ways. All types of assistance may be required before Muslims can be drafted in for the most serious goals. For example, knowing how to make Muslims a united voice to force the authorities in granting them their Islamic demands is a form of *i'dad*. The readying process or preparation differs in how it is presented and how it is run in the Muslim community itself. It can also differ completely in how it is run from lobbying to intimidation of authorities.

The readying process requires formation of systems that demand the need for scholars who have the ability to explain. They are to be

---

42 http://www.alaswaq.net/articles/2007/09/09/10655.html

skilled in expounding the doctrines and most importantly, they have the charisma to indoctrinate their listeners. And if those scholars cannot be local then itinerant ones may be used.

The readying process requires the formation of links to establish trusts with the local host community so that they would become local and ultimately speak on behalf of the Muslim community. These links are essentially keys to the survival of those Muslims in the host community. For instance the Muslim community makes mass promises to give its vote to a certain political party for returned favour. The Muslim community leader orders its members to buy their daily needs from certain places, thus making the very survival of that outlet dependent on the Muslim community. Obviously these links could be financial, political or the provision of whatever is deemed necessary to gain a foothold.

This would guarantee a favourable response from such quarters creating a deliberate confusion among the host society. For example: an attack has taken place in Amsterdam, those in Rotterdam would be saying, "Yes, we know an attack has taken place in Amsterdam but the Muslims here in Rotterdam are the most peaceful and friendly". This ultimately confuses the masses and conditions them to a state of **no action** or of indifference. The end result and the general conclusion would be that there may be a few misguided Muslims in Amsterdam, but those we have here in Rotterdam are peaceful.

The readying process requires sponsors, plus finding ways and means to infiltrate, but beyond that it requires the creation of rallying points and issues that can be used to attract attention. The focus would be on denial of some rights or correcting an oversight but with an unquestionable path being paved for further Islamisation and surrender on the part of the non-Muslim host society and the authorities. Consequently local issues are nationalised and national issues are globalised.

But to achieve all that and to find the people to induct, there must be immigration. And, not just any immigration but Muslim immigration, because all the foregoing preparation and battles are directly related to the immigration, for without immigration there would be no access to the installations of the enemy. Without the understanding and embracing the purity of the Islamic faith and the notion of its superior system, one would not be able to tear down the societal infrastructure of the enemy.

This 'readying' concept is Qur'anically prescribed and it is so important that Allah even took the trouble to spell it out with quite a few directives in the Qur'an itself. Let's first examine the Qur'anic reference Sura 8:60:

> "And make ready against them, all you can of power, including steeds of war (tanks, planes, missiles, artillery, etc.) to threaten the enemy of Allah and your enemy, and others besides whom, you may not know but whom Allah does know. And whatever you shall spend in the Cause of Allah shall be repaid unto you, and you shall not be treated unjustly."

Explaining the readying concept, Sheikh Ibn Baz[43], who was a leading international Islamic scholar and the grand *mufti* of Saudi Arabia, stated that the secrecy of the preparation is implicit and has to be taken seriously. Thus, there is the training with all sorts of weapons, the readying not only of heart and head but every bit of oneself. He goes on to say that one ought to become acquainted with every kind of warfare, for one doesn't know if one will be involved in a defensive or offensive *jihad*. What kind of weapons — land, sea or air weapons will be required? One has to be prepared and yet behave as though one had nothing. One has to be very deceptive about it. For the prophet said, 'War is deception.' Baz goes on to illustrate that most battles are not won by superiority of weapons but by the subtleties of deception, which requires a lot of skill to confuse the enemy with deceptive tactics.

I'dad is not just one thing, that is, to be able to carry weapons or to be able to use them. According to Dr. Ali Muhammad Al Sallabi[44],

---

[43] http://www.binbaz.org.sa/index.php?pg=mat&type=article&id=528
[44] Tabseer Al Mu'meneen bi Fiqh A'Naser wa Al Tamkeen fi Al Qur'an Al Karim

i'dad is sub-divided into stages and is a gradual process. He goes into details expounding the various stages of infiltration, gaining confidence, and the process of conditioning the opponents of Islam with an aim to weaken them[45].

Also, Al Shahari[46] explains that naturally the *tamkeen* of *i'dad* cannot be achieved overnight; but it has a prescribed process. He makes clear to his readers that the process has to be built upon from the basic to the most brutal form of *i'dad*, which he calls the stages of *tamkeen*[47].

The most important requirement of *i'dad* is the quantity or multiplication of numbers.

I'dad comes from the word *a'dad* meaning 'to number' or to count. Muslim scholars have referred to this as multiplication of their numbers — the greater their number, the greater the probability of establishment and the higher the chances of influence and takeover.

The whole issue of the enablement and the preparation paired with immigration and *jihad* was clearly spelled out by a Turkish journalist[48] when he said in his interview with a German newspaper, "You Germans think that we Turks are coming to Germany only seeking employment and to gather the crumbs of your money. No, we are coming here to take over your country and to be established in it and then to build what we see appropriate and all that with your approval and according to your laws."

This issue of increase in the numbers of Muslims is now a known norm in Western Europe. Demographic studies show that in twenty years time if the indigenous populations do not increase their birth rate, then the Muslims will be the majority in most of the Western European countries. It is not an issue of fertility but a clear plan as required and prescribed by the doctrine of *i'dad*.

---

[45] http://www.islamtoday.net/articles/show_articles_content.cfm?id=177&catid=191&artid=7135

[46] Awameel A'Naseer wa al Tamkeen fi Dawat Al Mursaleen

[47] http://mahawer.al-islam.com/dawaBooks/078.doc

[48] http://www.elaph.com/ElaphWriter/2004/11/23948.htm

Furthermore, the recognition of Muslim polygamous marriages by European governments means that the acceleration of their numbers is beyond all reasonable calculations.

Tamkeen and its goals

So *tamkeen* in its various forms has one objective and that is to gain power or the ability to rule. If that is not possible then the next ideal would be to dictate rules and regulations that would be in favour of Islam, thus curtailing all criticism of Islam. This would include saturating the society with an Islamic 'colour' by imposing and making the *Shariah* supreme and dominantly imposed within every aspect of the society especially in the socio-political sphere.

All the foregoing in regard to the Islamic doctrine of *Hijra* (immigration) and its various sub-sections of empowerment – *tamkeen* and its various divisions — are not merely human ideas or plans. But all of it is a divine promise and enablement of Muslims and their victory on earth by Allah.

The Qur'an declares this clearly in Sura 24:55,

> "Allah has promised those among you who believe, and do righteous good deeds, that He will certainly grant them succession to (the present rulers) in the earth, as He granted it to those before them, and that He will grant them the authority to practice their religion, that which He has chosen for them (i.e. Islam). And He will surely give them in exchange a safe security after their fear (provided) they (believers) worship Me and do not associate anything (in worship) with Me. But whoever disbelieved after this, they are the rebellious, disobedient to Allah."

This concept of taking over is regularly talked about by the Muslim scholars and declared openly. So, for instance, Sheikh Yousif Al Qardawi[49] has repeatedly said that the future is with Islam and it will

---

[49] http://www.islamonline.net/fatwa/arabic/FatwaDisplay.asp?hFatwaID=2042

outshine and out do and win over all other religions. Qardawi based his *fatwa* on what Muhammad's statement that when the Muslims take over Constantinople then they will win over Rome. He goes on to talk about Islam taking the whole of Europe. For Muhammad, the Prophet of Islam, promised his companions the treasures of Persia, Syria, Egypt, and Yemen, as well as conquering Rome[50]. So in Islam the conquest of Rome is a divine promise. Therefore, the Muslims will do all they can to achieve the takeover of Rome, and Rome symbolically means Europe. That is why the Muslims are so keen to take over Europe.

---

50 وخرج رسول الله فأخذ رداءه وجلس قال سلمان يا رسول الله رأيتك حين ضربت ما تضرب الضربة إلا كانت معها برقة قال له رسول الله يا سلمان رأيت ذلك فقال أي والذي بعثك بالحق يا رسول الله قال فإني حين ضربت الضربة الأولى رفعت لي مدائن كسرى وما حولها ومدائن كثيرة حتى رأيتها بعيني قال له من حضره من أصحابه يا رسول الله ادع الله أن يفتحها علينا ويغنمنا ديارهم ويخرب بأيدينا بلادهم فدعا رسول الله بذلك ثم ضربت الضربة الثانية فرفعت لي مدائن قيصر وما حولها حتى رأيتها بعيني قالوا يا رسول الله ادع الله أن يفتحها علينا ويغنمنا ديارهم ويخرب بأيدينا بلادهم فدعا رسول الله بذلك ثم ضربت الثالثة فرفعت لي مدائن الحبشة وما حولها من القرى حتى رأيتها بعيني قال رسول الله عند ذلك دعوا الحبشة ما ودعوكم واتركوا الترك ما تركوكم.
سنن النسائي (المجتبى) كتاب الجهاد باب غزوة الترك والحبشة. حديث رقم 3176
فكسر ثلثها، وقال: "الله أكبر، أعطيت مفاتيح الشام، والله إني لأبصر قصورها الحمراء من مكاني هذا". ثم ضرب الثانية فقطع الثلثالآخر فقال: "الله أكبر، أعطيت مفاتيح فارس، والله إني لأبصر قصر المدائن أبيض". ثم ضرب الثالثة وقال: "بسم الله" فقطع بقية الحجر فقال: "الله أكبر، أعطيت مفاتيح اليمن، والله إني لأبصر أبواب صنعاء من مكاني هذا الساعة". (2 رواه أحمد 303/4 وقال ابن حجر: إسناده حسن، انظر: الفتح 458/7
http://www.iid-alraid.de/EnOfQuran/Subject/00001/00002/00017/00040/00096.htm

POLITICAL TACTICS AND RELIGIOUS EMIGRATION

It is by now abundantly clear that one needs to look into the original *Hijra* of Muhammad by examining his techniques in order to understand the modern immigration tactics to the West in particular.

What has become clear from the foregoing is that Islamic planning regarding their migration is twofold:

(a) Long term strategy that will continue the immigration.

(b) Short term plans to back the long term strategy by working out the mechanism and time needed to achieve the goals of immigration.

One is bound to ask, was all this in the mind of Muhammad while he was considering migration to Yathrib/Medina?

In other words, as we examine Muhammad's plans and how he paced himself, an important question poses itself: did he have a strategy of some sort, a reasonably clear plan, or was it all chance and good illuminations at critical times which saved the day for him?

If it was a strategy, then what was it, and how do we know that we are not just guessing it? But if it was all to be illumination and mere chances or luck as some may call it, then there is nothing to investigate.

We think it was a strategy that he laid down, for he had many enemies and he worked out a system of how to take them down and subdue them, having isolated them, building careful alliance with warring factions and then managing them with master political manipulations. It is time to reflect back.

Was he inspired to move to Yathrib — which he later renamed Medina? Or was it a calculated strategy?

Muhammad's self-declaration of his prophetic call in Mecca to the Quraish was met with strong opposition. Under pressure from his followers he granted them permission to seek refuge in Abyssinia. While desiring to settle his differences with the Quraish he decided to make a concession to them by compromising a central doctrinal issue. One day when he was at the *Ka'aba* and looked around, to his surprise he saw most of the leaders of the major clans there. While reciting a Sura — which appears today as Sura 53 — he claimed to have received a new revelation. In his recitation at the *Ka'aba* he now acknowledged the idols of the Quraish in an elevated status equal in power of intercession with Allah. This pleased all the pagan Meccans and they bowed with him. But the problem arose when his followers questioned him if that were true, and if it was, were they, his followers, guilty as they had destroyed their idols? And if it was true, why did he not say it a bit earlier? For then their kinsmen and families would have not needed to make that arduous journey through the desert — one in which some never reached their destination. Muhammad was caught on all sides. He in turn managed to convince them that it wasn't he as he was just as puzzled as they were. His usual answer was that he would inquire of the angel who was bringing him the revelations. The next day he rose to tell them that they were 'satanic verses' as Satan had managed to imitate the voice of Gabriel the angel while Gabriel was waiting for Muhammad to catch his breath, as Muhammad was listening and reciting it simultaneously.

This complicated the matter on both sides, and, though some of his followers doubted, he managed to win those that really mattered from his own. But the Quraish was lost as the explanation of satanic verses meant that their religion was satanic and had nothing to do with his new revelation. And due to his denial and renouncing of what he had uttered on the previous day, the Quraish felt betrayed and cheated. This led to serious accusations, making Muhammad's position even more precarious. Nevertheless, he was able to weather the storm as he had a dual protection in the person of his wife Khadija and his uncle Abu Talib. Both of them were in leadership roles of the city. Added to that, Abu Talib was one of the leading elders and in a position of authority in Mecca. Without his permission none could harm Muhammad. Muhammad's uncle Abu Talib had given Muhammad his support publicly to speak whatever he desired, privately he had asked him to tone his message down.

In 620AD Muhammad's uncle and wife Khadija died within a short time of each other. Muslim scholars differ on whether it was ten days or three months. Nevertheless, Muhammad was vulnerable and soon his enemies rose with a threefold plan either to imprison him, kill him or to send him away in exile. This was public news although Muhammad claimed that Allah revealed to him their plans:

> Sura 8:30 "And (remember) when the disbelievers plotted against you (O Muhammad to imprison you, or to kill you, or to get you out (from your home, i.e. Makkah); they were plotting and Allah too was plotting, and Allah is the Best of the plotters."

In the face of this critical development Muhammad needed to move fast, so he approached some of the key tribal leaders seeking refuge and protection from Quraish. He was turned down by every one of them. Muhammad realised that they turned him down as they were bound in an alliance with the Quraish and their livelihood depended on appeasing the Quraish tribe.

So he decided to immigrate to an oasis town called Ta'if that was not too far away from Mecca. Ta'if was inhabited by Jews and Arabs. The Thakif /Sakif was a large and influential Arab tribe and it seems that Muhammad knew them and might have had dealings in the past with them from his business days. Muhammad, accompanied by his adopted son Ziad ibn Harith, arrived in Ta'if only to be chased out of the town with some brutality, so he had no choice but to return back to Mecca. The reason Ta'if hounded and chased Muhammad out of their town was not only because of security concerns but it was proclaimed to be the home town of Allaat, one of the main goddesses of Quraish. There was a regular flow of pilgrims and Ta'if had an excellent climate for rich fruit orchards. As such, it was a destination for most of the wealthy Meccans during the hot summers. Thus Ta'if stood to lose a lot if they were to grant Muhammad refuge in their town.

His official biographies state that he begged them not to inform the Quraish, but they did. By the time he reached Mecca, the news had preceded him, and he was unable to access the town for fear of his life. However, the biographers went on to state that he had sent a messenger with a plea to Mu'ta'eam bin Adi, one of leading notables of Mecca and member of the board of elders, to extend his protection to Muhammad. Ibn Adi having agreed to protect him, Muhammad spent that night at Ibn Adi's house. The next morning the host and the guest went out together for all to see that Muhammad was now a protégé of Ibn Adi, thus safe and beyond harm of the Quraish.

We have looked and examined very carefully the different *Sira* or biographical accounts of Muhammad's life compiled by various Muslim scholars. There are some important observations that we have gleaned from them:

1. Muhammad's trip to Ta'if was undertaken in utmost secrecy. Virtually none of the Muslim community knew his real intentions and plans.

2. Muhammad had managed to create a secure network of informants. These are known and referred to in the *Siras* or his biographies as Al-'Uyoun[51], meaning 'the eyes who watched', and reported everything, be it of value or not, to Muhammad. The Muslim scholars of the *Sira* of Muhammad mention some of those who were Al-'Uyoun, those being Sa'ad bin Ma'az, Sa'ad bin Ibada, Abduallah bin Ruwaha and Khawat bin Jubiae'r.

---

[49] Anwar fi siriat a'nabi al mukhtar by sulieman bin Muhammad Al lihimed http://www.almotaqeen.net/ Saad bin Ma'az, sa'ad bin Ibada, Abduallah bin Ruwaha, Khawat bin Jubiar, those were ala'eyoun

3. He also had carved out a secure communication system engaging sources from within the Muslim community and other sympathisers. This is because when Muhammad was hurt in Ta'if and he had managed to raise the alarm, he had one of his messengers, Khazia, to go and seek help from Ibn Adi; the rest of the commotion of activities clearly illustrates the point that has just been made. Without those things in place he could not have managed to move that swiftly.

4. This means that Muhammad had clearly thought out the various scenarios and had put alternative plans in place for all different outcomes. As a result, when he was turned away, he activated the 'help' plan.

5. In other words though outwardly it may seem that an organised state system came into being for the first time in Medina yet the truth is that it was already in place in some subtle form. It is clear from this and other incidents that Muhammad had a lot of underground systems up and running such as informants, private security, communication links, supply routes, financiers, etc.

The stark thing is that Ibn Adi lived and died as a *kaffir*, a non-Muslim — yet he protected Muhammad. There are nuances — and only nuances — that the provision of protection was due to mutual 'interests.' There were benefits on both sides, so protection was offered by Ibn Adi in exchange for Muhammad's help. Though some have been mentioned, none of the sources are authentic and it would be inappropriate to speculate. What is important to notice is that he used the *darura'* (necessity) as well as the *tayseer* (easing the burden) principle.

Muhammad was prepared to overlook Ibn Adi's unbelief, steeped in paganism. He overlooked his uncle Abu Talib, and so once again the *darura'* principle! This principle is much deeper than most people realise. Somehow it is quite amazing that when Muhammad was seeking refuge in Ta'if he was running away from one set of *kafirs* (apostate pagans) to another (we will revisit this principle later). This has become an important principle for today's *Mujahedeen* who are wanted terrorists in their homelands. They have run away from those *kafirs*, seeking refuge with the European or Western *kafirs*. This is with a determination that from the safety of Europe, they will be targeting both their homelands as well as their new adopted homes.

What happened? How did Muhammad manage to stay in Mecca? What was his relationship with the Quraish until his migration to Medina?

It is thought that this was one of the busiest periods of his life. First Muhammad married Sa'wada a widow of a Muslim refugee who had immigrated to Abyssinia. Next, he also married Aisha, daughter of his best friend Abu Baker, who was then only 6 years old. That means on the social front he was settled and prosperous as his business continued. In fact the turnover of Khadija's business was formidable. It has been said that her business monthly turnover was equivalent to a whole year's balance for the entire tribe of Quraish. It might have dwindled but it was there and must have been enough to make him comfortable. Otherwise he would have been frantically worried about his life. As for the persecution it could be that the Muslim biographers might have exaggerated it beyond all proportion.

For us, the most important aspect of these two years before Muhammad's *Hijra* is to know how Muhammad spent them gathering information about Yathirb, the next town that he was planning to go to and which he renamed Medinatu al Nabi "the city of the prophet" which is popularly known as Medina.

THE SETTING AT YATHRIB/MEDINA

Yathrib was a distinctly Jewish city. There were two Arab tribes, Aws and Khazraj. The Khazraj were related to banu Al Najar who in turn were the nephews of Muhammad from the side of his mother Ameenah and they were also related to his grandfather Abdel Muttalib. Thus, Muhammad had some strong family ties to the Jewish city of Yathrib. Of course, the Jews considered Yathrib to be a Jewish city as they had established it. But the Arab tribes, the Aws, and the Khazraj were seeking to claim the city for themselves.

In the struggle for power and taking control of the city, the Aws and the Khazraj had entered separately into independent alliances with the different Jewish tribes who had their own power structures clearly established.

What might have interested Muhammad most were the grievances that the people of Yathrib had against the Quraish. Yathrib was the leading commercial city in Arabia but when the Zamzam well was found and water was no longer in shortage, Mecca became the main caravan route as a stopping and refuelling post. Aws and Khazraj were anxious to break the superior hold that the Jews had in Yathrib and that of the Quraish further afield in Mecca.

Seeking alliances with 15 Arab[52] tribes

Ibn Hisham and Ibn Katheer (both of whom are recognised as authentic biographers of Muhammad), state that Muhammad had

---

[52] Abkar Al sakaf A'deen fi al jazeera al arabiya.bab arad a'nabi Nafsahu ala Kabaeel

appealed to some 15 Arab tribes[53] to grant him protection but none would have him, due to their ties with Quraish. So he had now set his eyes on Yathrib and was exploring how to approach that option.

It was at this time some six men from the Aws came to Mecca from Yathrib in 620AD seeking to make an alliance with Quraish against the Khazraj. When Muhammad learned of their presence in Mecca he looked them up and managed to influence them and diverted them from forming that alliance. The six men also happened to be Muhammad's distant maternal relatives.

In 621AD some 12 men, (6 from the Aws and 6 from the Khazraj) came and made the first pledge to Muhammad, at Aqaba glen[54], known as the 'Pledge of Aqaba.' Muhammad charged them to abstain from vulgarity and to adhere to the Qur'an.

In 622AD some 75 more from the Aws and Khazraj came. However, some scholars say there were 72 men and 3 women who made the second pledge of Aqaba. So now it was agreed that Muhammad and his followers would discreetly leave Mecca and immigrate to Medina.

During the two years that Muhammad spent in Mecca under the protection of Ibn Adi, he sent some of his key followers to Medina/Yathrib. These men taught what was so far revealed of the Qur'an to these new converts who were also instructed to watch and gather information. Muhammad's followers travelled quietly to and fro while Muhammad made meticulous calculations on every side. He investigated the various factors and situations of the power structures and all that he could gather about the society in Medina.

Musa'ab was one of those who travelled to and fro. Surprisingly enough, as all the religious duties including prayer were legislated in Medina there was not much to teach except that Allah had sent Muhammad as the last messenger. But regarding instructed practices, nothing was yet revealed. All the duties or so-called Pillars of Islam

---

[53] دعوة محمد بعض القبائل إلى دعوته

[54] http://www.al-eman.com/Islamlib/viewchp.asp?BID=251&CID=42#s4

were revealed later on in Medina. So the main thrust was to put up Muhammad as a viable leader. Of course, there were no miracles to report either, so the unifying grounds revolved around the enmity of the Quraish and support for Muhammad[55].

At the same time his condemnation of the Quraish became harsher. Furthermore, Muhammad increasingly began to recite favourable reve- lations towards to the Jews. This is clear from the Qur'an because all the pro-Jewish revelations are dated to this period. The more Muham- mad began to plan his migration, the stronger his 'revelations' favour- ing the Jews became. These revelations almost convinced the Jews that they had nothing to fear. He was sending a signal to the Jews that although he was coming at the invitation of the Aws and the Khazraj, unlike his hosts he believed in their scriptures (i.e. Torah and Psalms); and as a result, the Jews had hoped and thought that the rest of Muslims would follow in this belief. Muhammad persuaded the Jews that the balance of power would remain the same under his leader- ship. In fact, if anything at all, it would increase in the favour of the Jews as his revelations were pointing to the fact that they, the Jews, were chosen above all. And as chosen people, most of the prophets had come from the Jews, etc. and the Qur'an was a mere Arabic version of what they held. So Muhammad laid a deceptive masterplan to give the Jews a sense of false security lest they side with the Quraish and refuse him as the people of Ta'if had done.

Muhammad was determined that under no circumstances would the Jews of Yathrib, trading partners with the Quraish, even dream of handing him back. There would be no repeat of Ta'if. In other words, he was closing every loophole that could have been there in order to gain favour and support from the Jews.

This was an alliance of convenience and mutual benefit. The Arabs were envious of the Jews since they were prosperous, had a clear reli- gion, prophets, and even a revealed book. All that the Jews possessed

---

[55] Sirat ibn kathir vol 2 page 352, section Pledge of Aqqaba I, & II, Sirat Ibn Hisham, vol 2, page 454, Bayat al Aqqaba wa Rijaleha

gave them a certain status that the Arabs wanted. The Arabs had no prophet, no book and no real religion, but they thought that through Muhammad they would receive the exemplary status they were seeking. The Aws and the Khazraj were constantly at war with each other but they desired to unite in order to break that Jewish supremacy. However, they did not have the ability to do so.

Muhammad also knew that the Jewish power and influence extended far beyond Yathrib, so he deployed the doctrines of *muda'rat / takkiya*, and *darura'* in order to pave a way between the Jews and Muhammad.

Muda'rat[56] مداراة

Muda'rat is a *Sunni* doctrine of deception. It is also another name for *takkiya*. Not many people know about this doctrine outside the circles of the *Ulama* or the learned scholars of Islam.

Muda'rat simply means flattery, adulation, conformity with, deceit, trickery, keeping pace with, wrap, conceal or hide. This deceptive behaviour can be practiced with anybody when necessary. However, the *Sunni* Scholars have identified ten categories of people who are to be regularly targeted by *Muda'rat*:

1. *Kaffir* (a non-Muslim)
2. A tyrannical ruler
3. Those whose hearts have been recently reconciled to Islam (new converts to Islam)
4. One who has deviated from the truth of Islam to win him back
5. A Muslim who has gone astray in imitating the non-believers
6. A learned scholar or scientist to benefit from his knowledge
7. A friend
8. One's enemies

---

[56] http://www.islamadvice.com/nasiha/nasiha160.htm

9. One's spouse

10. A person who may be ill (by giving him hope that he will be well and looks well, for example).

The *Sunni* Scholars have focused on various Qur'anic texts justifying their position. Their main examples have been all the prophets who lied as practicing *Muda'rat* like Ibrahim (Abraham), Mariam (Mary, Mother of Jesus), Shu'aib (an Arabian prophet) and even Muhammad the prophet of Islam.

Ibrahim lied as per Sura 21:51–66,

> 51 We bestowed aforetime on Abraham his rectitude of conduct, and well were We acquainted with him.
>
> 52 Behold! he said to his father and his people, "What are these images, to which ye are (so assiduously) devoted?"
>
> 53 They said, "We found our fathers worshipping them."
>
> 54 He said, "Indeed ye have been in manifest error — ye and your fathers."
>
> 55 They said, "Have you brought us the Truth, or are you one of those who jest?"
>
> 56 He said, "Nay, your Lord is the Lord of the heavens and the earth, He Who created them (from nothing): and I am a witness to this (Truth).
>
> 57 "And by Allah, I have a plan for your idols — after ye go away and turn your backs".
>
> 58 So he broke them to pieces, (all) but the biggest of them, that they might turn (and address themselves) to it.
>
> 59 They said, "Who has done this to our gods? He must indeed be some man of impiety!"
>
> 60 They said, "We heard a youth talk of them: He is called Abraham."
>
> 61 They said, "Then bring him before the eyes of the people, that they may bear witness."

62 They said, "Art thou the one that did this with our gods, O Abraham?"

63 He said: "Nay, this was done by — this is their biggest one! ask them, if they can speak intelligently!"

64 So they turned to themselves and said, "Surely ye are the ones in the wrong!"

65 Then were they confounded with shame: (they said), "Thou knowest full well that these (idols) do not speak!"

66 (Abraham) said, "Do ye then worship, besides Allah, things that can neither be of any good to you nor do you harm?"

Mariam/Mary told to lie as per Sura 19:25-26,

25 "And shake towards thyself the trunk of the palm-tree: It will let fall fresh ripe dates upon thee.

26 "So eat and drink and cool (thine) eye. And if thou dost see any man, say, 'I have vowed a fast to (Allah) Most Gracious, and this day will I enter into not talk with any human being'"

27 At length she brought the (babe) to her people, carrying him (in her arms). They said: "O Mary! truly an amazing thing hast thou brought!"

Bukhari reports in *Hadith* no. 5780 that the Prophet said, "We must deal with our enemies with smiles on our faces and curses in our hearts."

Muhammad went on to say, *"War is deception"*. This deception can be practiced at a personal level as well as at a community level through its leaders and institutions. Please check *The Mosque Exposed* (Qur'anic injunctions for a viable survival *takiyya*) by the same authors.

Muhammad practiced *takiyya* by claiming new revelations all in the favour of the Jews. He said that they are the chosen people of Allah, relating the stories of most of their prophets using their religious terminology, etc., and that he was in the line of those prophets now sent to the Arabian people. But while claiming all those revelations in favour of the Jews his intentions were very different. This is shown by the content of his pact with the Aws and the Khazraj. For it was radically opposite to all what he was pretending to be saying to the Jews.

Ibn Ishaq[57], reports in his *Sira* that the pledge of loyalty made by the 75 men was an extraordinary pledge. It was not a religious pledge of loyalty for preaching and proclaiming Muhammad's message but it was a military pact to fight, kill or subdue the 'red and black' as Muhammad stated it, with red meaning the Jews, and black meaning the Quraish.

Pledge of war

On the night of the pledge, very secretly and discreetly Muhammad left Mecca with his uncle Abbas bin Abdel Muttalib. Abbas knew that this alliance was an alliance of War. When they — the Aws and the Khazraj — had all gathered to pledge loyalty, Abbas (Muhammad's uncle) spoke first. He asked them if they knew what they were supporting or what they were pledging their loyalty for. They responded by saying that they knew what they were supporting. Muhammad's uncle continued to inform the men that they were pledging their loyalty to fight the red (Jews) and the black (the unbelievers of Mecca, i.e. Quraish and all the other Meccan tribes) people. The men were told, "So if you think that you have risked your wealth and your elders to be killed unnecessarily, then hand him over. If you do so, then by Allah this would be shameful forever. But if you see that you are amenable to making this pledge of war with loyalty to Allah, sharing wealth, killing the so-called nobles then you are the best of this world and hereafter."

After Abbas made them aware of what they were just about to do, Muhammad then spoke and said that by undertaking them, he was to

---

[57] http://www.al-eman.com/Islamlib/viewchp.asp?BID=249&CID=30 and
http://sirah.al-islam.com/Display.asp?f=msr10064

prohibit himself from doing what they would forbid their wives and their children from doing. So one of the delegates, Al Barra', took Muhammad's hand in his own and said:

> "By the one who has sent you as a prophet, we will forbid you what we forbid our own, we pledge allegiance to you O apostle of Allah but we are the children of war, and the family of a warring clan, we have inherited this from generation after generation".

At this point Abu Haitham interjected saying:

> "O apostle of Allah, between us and the Jews are ropes (meaning ties or links) and we are about to cut those and if we do that, then we might have disobeyed being in breach of our own agreement with them and so Allah may show you to come back to your people?"

This was very clever of him, as he stated clearly that they were about to cut the ropes — meaning the relationship — that they had with the Jews. They all probably knew that the so-called new revelations in favour of the Jews were just a gimmick or a decoy, but wanted to be absolutely certain. Abu Haitham was saying that if then their enmity with the Jews might be considered inappropriate, then the messenger of Allah may change his mind and return back to Mecca! If that were to be the case, then the Aws and the Khazraj would be incurring a double loss for they would have lost the relationship with the Jews as well as that with Quraish having given Muhammad a refuge in their town.

Muhammad smiled and said, "Blood, blood destruction, destruction." This meant a declaration of war and killing and destruction. In other words, Muhammad was saying, behold I have settled the fate of the Jews. They are going to be annihilated and so will I get rid of the Quraish. The old order will be fully done away with and I will establish a new order... Listen to what he said next:

> "I am of you and you are of me, I will fight (war) with those that you are (fighting) in war with, and I will make peace

with those you will make peace with. See I am of you and you are of me, your enemies are mine and I will fight them, and those whom you make peace with I will make peace."

Amazingly, even though Muhammad claimed to be a prophet, he set forth no principles, no conditions, no revelations and no sanctions from Allah over this deal. On the contrary, he went alongside the proposal of eliminating the Jews and the Quraish. This proves the very point on which the alliance and migration was based, shaped and had a whole political mark. Muhammad, who claimed to receive revelations from Allah regarding the most trivial of issues, had nothing to offer. All he did was accept and go alongside the tabled proposal(s). So Al-Bar and the rest of them[58] were so joyful and they made an allegiance to Muhammad.

It is clear from the wording of the second 'Pledge of Aqaba' that the decision was taken to fight the Quraish and the Jews with the aim of either total conversion or submission. Thus Muhammad had spelled out his decision which sealed and settled the fate of the Jews long before he ever reached Yathrib. However, when he first arrived in Yathrib, he made a public pretence of getting close to the Jews and befriending them, praying in the direction of Jerusalem, and fasting with them. He even included them in his first Charter of Medina, which stipulated a fraternal relationship with each other among the Aws, Khazraj and the new immigrants from Mecca. He also declared enmity with the Quraish declaring them outlaws. Including the Jews as a party in the charter was an ingenious plan that allowed Muhammad to manage them effectively without disclosing his real intentions. Interestingly, today's Muslim proponents and intellectuals glamorise the Medina Charter as the true illustration of Islam's multi-ethnic pluralism and acceptance of non-Muslims in their midst.

The Jewish elders' public support for the Charter meant that they were now in enmity with the Quraish. Otherwise they would be

---

[58] http://www.al-eman.com/Islamlib/viewchp.asp?BID=249&CID=30 and http://sirah.al-islam.com/Display.asp?f=msr10064

conducting a double life, for it was an either/or situation. Later on and because of their trade and other strategic interests, they would be forced to reinstate their relationship with the Quraish or respond to their pleas for help. Either way this was ultimately going to provide the legitimacy of the brutality that met them by the Muslims under Muhammad. That's exactly what took place with one Jewish tribe after another.

The clear fact was that the fate of the Jews had been decided upon even before Muhammad ever reached Yathrib. This 'example' by Muhammad, i.e. his *Sunnah*, has defined the fate of the non-Islamic host society facing the Muslim immigrant as they grow in power. The time factor may vary but the ultimate outcome is known.

Setting the goals

As we see, it was clear to Muhammad that his mission and the potentiality of his followers were being hampered in Mecca. He needed to go some place where both of these factors would enable him to extend the sphere of his influence by establishing an Islamic community from an Islamic state. He also realised the strategic location of Yathrib with the presence of a strong Jewish constituency and all the resources they owned. If he could overtake Yathrib, it would enhance his mission. So outwardly he was giving assurances to the Jews, yet inwardly he was planning their demise. This point is very clear when he gave his word to Heitham and the delegation from Yathrib about his loyalty to them.

His techniques for asserting his authority despite contradictions

By now Muhammad had successfully convinced his followers of gradual or progressive revelations. He had also managed to introduce two other doctrines that made no sense: the doctrine of abrogation and doctrine of *takiyya/ muda'rat*. Through these doctrines, he managed to move his followers from one position to another: from the

Jews being a chosen people and the people of the book to now being the worshippers of a calf, disobedient to Moses. Thus, the Jews now were in enmity with Allah. So even today, all Jews are considered the same as their predecessors. They are enemies of Allah and of his messenger and therefore personal enemies of the believers too. The Muslim mindset is that Jews must be fought against and nothing less than a total annihilation of them will do.

Establishment of a formidable infrastructure

To demonstrate the importance of mosques, Muhammad built one on his arrival even before he built his house. Amazingly his 'ministry' in Mecca spanned some 13 years but he never built a mosque there. This was something new: it was a declaration of authority. From that point on, the mosque was to be used not only for ritual prayers and religious teaching, but so much more. A mosque was to be:

1. Central to the life of a Muslim community

2. Civil as well as religious building

3. A court as well as class room

4. A military as well as mission base

5. A place of commendations as well as condemnations.

Of course, having built the Medina mosque, Muhammad also introduced a prayer call which was to become a tool of discrimination in the sense that later on having claimed to have received a revelation to humiliate the Jews and the Christians, their shofars and church bells were silenced.

Today, the landscape of Europe, North and South America is rapidly changing as mosques spring up in almost every major city as well as towns and suburbs. Once the mosques are built, especially reflecting so-called Islamic architecture, it all becomes part of the Islamic *tamkeen* (empowerment) and the *i'dad* (multiplication). The readying effect of the increase in their numbers is a reality!

Following the example of Muhammad's charge, that is a five-fold principle to usher in Islam's utter superiority. This is through the gathering, the listening, the obeying, migrating and the *jihad*. All of Islam can and does take effect in a host society through these five principles or outlets.

TAMKEEN AND I'DAD LESSONS FROM MUHAMMAD'S MIGRATION

Having considered and understood the principles of Islamic migration and the various doctrines attached (*tamkeen, i'dad, tayseer, darura'* and *takiyya* or *mud'arat*), as well as having considered the migration of Muhammad from Mecca to Medina, his communication system of informers and his pre-determined pact with the Jews, we are now ready to compare and contrast the present-day Muslim community and their aspirations of establishing an Islamic society ruled by the *Shariah* in the heartland of Europe. So migration is ultimately a conquest and not a migration.

To understand the point of 'conquest' as opposed to 'migration' please refer to: *The Islamisation of Britain and what must be done to prevent it* by Colin Dye (Pilcrow Press Report September 2007). This report gives practical examples of how Muslims have implemented the principles of *tamkeen* and *i'dad* in the conquest of the UK with gradual progression towards the establishment of an Islamic supremacy, while the host society has remained unaware and all the time thinking that requests have only been for a few religious and cultural needs. In a democratic society these types of requests are seen as valid and legitimate and are ultimately granted.

Mosques

By popular view mosques are regarded by most people simply as places of worship, not knowing that it isn't fully so. Mosques usually start out in a home then they are moved to a warehouse or perhaps in some rented accommodation. Then permission is sought for a licensed building to be used as a mosque. Then comes the first purpose-built mosque. Once one mosque is established then the mushrooming of the mosques continues and there is no way to stop that in a democratic society.

Mosques are at the heart of the community. The mosque is the most crucial infrastructure for the development of any Muslim community. Building mosques is a strategy to emulate and imitate Muhammad.

Of course, to make it viable, Muslims are asked to congregate and to be able to attend regularly. They are encouraged to live close by. Soon the community changes, expands and moves outward a few miles down the road. And they go on with the same tactics until the whole town is Islamised.

Diet rules

Usually application is made for diet consideration. Diet rules are looked upon favourably and without a second thought. Therefore there is the demand for *halal* meat for families or for private consumption. What is not understood by both local and central government legislators is that a Muslim's diet *per se* is not a personal choice, it is part of the *Shariah* which comes under *ibadat* (religious observances and regulations). The mosque also comes under *ibadat*. So does the *hijab* and so does *jihad*.

But permission is sought to show the reasonableness, tolerant nature of the new community and its law-abiding attitude. Were the experts to look into the Islamic request they would have discovered that as per the Qur'anic directive there is **no need for *halal* meat**. As the meat of the people of the Book is allowed and made lawful to the Muslims as per Sura 5:3,

> "Made lawful to you this day are [all kinds of (lawful) foods, which Allah has made lawful (meat of slaughtered eatable animals, etc., milk products, fats, vegetables and fruits, etc.). The food (slaughtered cattle, eatable animals,

etc.) of the people of the Scripture (Jews and Christians) is lawful to you and yours is lawful to them. (Lawful to you in marriage) are chaste women from the believers and chaste women from those who were given the Scripture (Jews and Christians) before your time, when you have given their due dowry (bridal money given by the husband to his wife at the time of marriage), desiring chastity (i.e. taking them in legal wedlock) not committing illegal sexual intercourse, nor taking them as girlfriends. And whosoever disbelieves in the Oneness of Allah and in all the other Articles of Faith [i.e. His (Allah's)]"

In other words the Qur'anic injunction states that meat slaughtered by Jews and Christians is lawful for a Muslim, so Sura 5:3 establishes the fact that our meat is *halal* to them. One wonders if their Imams and scholars ever looked at this verse? Of course, they have and they know it. They choose to overlook it deliberately as stated before. Here again the doctrine of *tamkeen* is implemented and there is a gradual process of establishing the Islamic identity in the host society.

From an *i'dad* point of view the demand for *halal* meat gives a Muslim community a voice at a social level and recognition by the government and food authority. At a legal and national level, this recognition would lead indirectly to further alienation, consolidating the segregation mode. Of course, if local supermarkets were to invest in making *halal* meat available then the commercial viability allows it to make even deeper inroads with the expansion of Islamic identity and the recognition of the *Shariah* through the back door so to speak!

Soon it would move from the personal need of the Muslims into the public places — it would be cumbersome to provide different kinds of meat at school meals, for example. And as the Muslims become the most vocal in their demands, they will be heard. So the school canteens would go *halal* to cater to the increasing number of Muslim children. If those canteens are run by an outside catering company they would be approached and it might just be in their interest if they are supplying the local hospital, local prison and other public amenities such as elderly homes, etc., to have all their meals as *halal* as a rule. For commercial companies the profit margin is their priority.

Hijab

The *hijab* like the *halal* meat comes under *ibadat*, the religious observations, and therefore is part of the Islamic *Shariah* as declared by Islamic scholars. While the *halal* meat is insidious the *hijab* is overt and an 'in your face' part of Islamic society. Of course, both *tamkeen* and *i'dad* are applied here too.

Implementation of the *hijab* has always been gradual. It would start as a headscarf and then move to a full garment with a headscarf. Then it would become the wearing of the *hijab* and finally the wearing of the *neqab*. (*Neqab* is fully covering the face with only two little holes for the eyes). By the time they reach the state of wearing the *neqab*, the society would have become so conditioned by it that no one would give it a second look or thought.

Shariah

Once mosques are erected, *da'wa* centres are up and running, Qur'anic schools are functioning, *halal* meat is being served in schools, hospitals, prisons and other public outlets, *hijab* is being accommodated and then the *Shariah* law is in full swing. It is not only to be limited to the Muslim community but is purposely aimed at impacting directly the host society (see Appendix B).

Naturally with the increase in the number of Muslim festival days and other religious celebrations being added to the public calendar, prayers are held publicly as a show of strength and declaration of Islamic identity. All of these practices are a must as they follow the example of exactly what Muhammad did in Medina. It is the silent imposition of Islam and the conditioning of the host society/people to get used to the Islamic buildings, dress and eating codes to the point that nobody would think twice about the whole subtle change of their own environment. In sum, the host society becomes indifferent to the religious, social and political tactics used to establish a totality of Islamic rule under *Shariah*. That was the conquest of Muhammad and is the impetus of Muslim migration today in every part of the world.

From henceforth demands would not stop. Islamic promoters would continue to look for issues as rallying points. No matter how insignificant the issues, they become blown out of proportion and taken to the national level. This strategy is skilfully managed in that sympathy is sought and help is gained from local and national political leaders and parties. They are in return promised the Muslim vote, etc.

Every local tradition of the host society is looked into and carefully examined to find ways and means of undoing it by challenging it in one way or another. Muslims either refuse to participate in it or they openly boycott it to demonstrate the difference and the separateness of the Muslim society.

Outwardly, it might look like they will end up losing but in fact only the opposite happens: they end up securing their demands even more insistently.

Muhammad changed the name of Yathrib to Medina (City of the Apostle) once there were enough conditioned people. And so in certain areas there come various proposals to change a host society. For example, the names of streets or major roads and routes are given new names and the community is told to use those new names. And as those become official addresses, they are soon accepted without recourse.

With all the Qur'anic schools, mosques and the *da'wa* centres springing up, one would have thought that Islamic educational schools are not needed. But those so-called 'faith schools' are political academies that ingrain the Islamic identity in the hearts and the minds of the young generation. Children and young adults are being raised then as tomorrow's leaders. Educational segregation is vital for the ultimate conquest and Islamisation of the host community.

Harmless changes with explosive potential

Muhammad made maximum use of what he called 'the doctrine of abrogation' having introduced it to overcome the debacle of the so-called 'satanic verses' incident. As stated earlier when he arrived in Yathrib/Medina to give the Jews a sense of security, he adopted some of their key religious practices such as fasting and praying in the direction toward Jerusalem.

When Muhammad was powerful enough to assert his identity long before he began the liquidation process of the Jewish tribes, he changed the direction of prayer and changed fasting from a few days to the whole month of Ramadan. At face value this seemed to be a harmless change only affecting religious dogma. In reality it was a whole shift in relationship and the identity of his new community in which they felt previously that there was more of a **common ground** between them and the Jews than with the Quraish.

Now that the new Muslim community realised that the *Ka'aba* and its surroundings were sacred Islamic sites they were more keen to liberate Mecca from the hands of the 'pagan Quraish' who were regarded as the enemies of Allah and his apostle Muhammad. The host society began to embrace the Arabian sites that were considered holy by the pagans. Hence, changing the direction of prayer was an inner preparation towards a hidden goal and inner breakup with the Jews. The Jews were also declared infidels since they ought to have known better — their *Qibla*, or direction of prayer, toward Jerusalem was a temporary one. Muhammad declared that Mecca was the true direction, for even Allah had revealed that to the Jews in their scriptures. The fact that Abraham himself with the help of his son Ishmael had built the *Ka'aba* being led by Allah,

> Sura 2:127: "And (remember) when Ibrahim (Abraham) and (his son) Isma'il (Ishmael) were raising the foundations of the House (the Ka'bah at Makkah), (saying), "Our Lord! Accept (this service) from us. Verily! You are the All-Hearer, the All-Knower."

Muhammad claimed that the Patriarch was shown and instructed to build this house *Ka'aba* in Mecca, as per Sura 2:125-126,

> "125 And (remember) when We made the House (the Ka'bah at Makkah) a place of resort for mankind and a place of safety. And take you (people) the place of Ibrahim (Abraham) [or the stone on which Ibrahim (Abraham) stood while he was building the Ka'bah] as a place of prayer (for some of your prayers, e.g. two Rak'at after the Tawaf of the Ka'bah at Makkah), and We commanded Ibrahim (Abraham) and Ismail (Ishmael) that they should purify My House (the Ka'bah at Makkah) for those who are circumambulating it, or staying, or bowing or prostrating themselves (there, in prayer).
>
> 126 And (remember) when Ibrahim (Abraham) said, "My Lord, make this city (Makkah) a place of security and provide its people with fruits, such of them as believe in Allah and the Last Day." He (Allah) answered: "As for him who disbelieves, I shall leave him in contentment for a while, then I shall compel him to the torment of the Fire, and worst indeed is that destination!"

This change therefore was not simply a minor religious dogma but a whole shift in attitude which was going to affect the implementation of what Muhammad had in his heart, that is, the liquidation of both Jews and the Quraish, and the utter and absolute dominion of Islam over both of them.

Having introduced these changes, the battle of Bader was a foregone conclusion for this was the readying process and the indoctrination was successful. Now it was launch time.

In a new environment and new non-Muslim society various factors are considered. These may be traditional practices; they may be values that might be even unspoken courtesies that are deeply embedded in the culture. But one after another is challenged in a seemingly innocent manner but with a firm plan to uproot the host society and consolidate the Islamic society gaining more power and dominion over the host society.

I'htiraz: precautionary principle

I'htiraz simply means to be careful, to be cautious, and to take precautionary steps. This principle is applied to every aspect of one's life from belief extending to one's own security to one's guard against one's enemies even when praying:

> Sura 4,102 "When thou (O Messenger) art with them, and standest to lead them in prayer, Let one party of them stand up (in prayer) with thee, Taking their arms with them: When they finish their prostrations, let them Take their position in the rear. And let the other party come up which hath not yet prayed — and let them pray with thee, Taking all precaution, and bearing arms: the Unbelievers wish, if ye were negligent of your arms and your baggage, to assault you in a single rush. But there is no blame on you if ye put away your arms because of the inconvenience of rain or because ye are ill; but take (every) precaution for yourselves. For the Unbelievers Allah hath prepared a humiliating punishment."

Or when suspecting or fearing disobedience from one's wife:

> Sura 4:34 "Men are the protectors and maintainers of women, because Allah has given the one more (strength) than the other, and because they support them from their means. Therefore the righteous women are devoutly obedient, and guard in (the husband's) absence what Allah would have them guard. As to those women on whose part ye fear disloyalty and ill-conduct, admonish them, refuse to share their beds, beat them ; but if they return to obedience, seek not against them Means (of annoyance): For Allah is Most High, great (above you all)."

Or desertion on part of those engaged in war with the enemy:

> Sura 8:58 "If you (O Muhammad) fear treachery from any people throw back (their covenant) to them (so as to be) on equal terms (that there will be no more covenant between you and them). Certainly Allah likes not the treacherous."

Muhammad was very careful to snuff out any possible opposition before it gathered momentum. This quelling of all forms of opposition was a serious policy sanctioned by Qur'anic doctrines. If anyone criticised him or raised a doubt about his prophetic claims or gossiped about him in any form or shape the punishment was death. Of course, later on it was all sanctioned by the Qur'an not to vex the prophet nor to raise one's voice over his voice:

> Sura 49:22 "O ye who believe! Raise not your voices above the voice of the Prophet, nor speak aloud to him in talk, as ye may speak aloud to one another, lest your deeds become vain and ye perceive not." And to offend the prophet was to commit blasphemy.

However, because in his early days while establishing himself in Yathrib Muhammad did not have the full authority, he resorted to quietly liquidating his enemies. This he did by rewarding those who assassinated his enemies publicly.

The liquidation of opponents

There was a Jewess called Asma bint Marwan who had given shelter to a blind man by the name of Umaeer bin Adi, and she would feed him every day. According to A'Nissai and Abu Dawud he was her partner and they had two sons. He converted to Islam, and this Jewess used to call Muhammad names. He asked her not to do so, but she continued, and so Umaeer authorised her killing. So one night when she was nursing her baby in bed, Umaeer came and pushed a spear in her stomach until it came out of her back. The baby fell at her legs.

The next day when Umaeer informed Muhammad what he had done Muhammad publicly commended him (Reported by ibn Taymiyah pages 95-96 Sareem al Maslul fi shatem a'rasul).

Then, there was an 80 year-old Um Qarefe' whose real name was Fatima bint Rubiya'a. She composed and recited a critical poem about Muhammad. She had 13 sons and they were all elders and Jewish tribal leaders. Because of her criticism of Muhammad, her feet were tied to two camels which walked in opposite directions, ultimately pulling her until she was torn into pieces. This punishment was carried out by Qayes bin Al Mushar who was ordered by Zaid bin Haritha (trajum al ama'al bab wafayat, fateh al bari bi sharah bi shahih al bukhari Kitab al maghazi, bab ghazawat zaid bin al haritha).

One hundred and twenty year-old Abu Afaq was a leader of the Jewish tribe of Banu Qunaiqa. When he heard of the killing of Quraish by Muhammad and his followers, he commented that if that was how relatives dealt with each other then there was no good left in life anymore. His comment was taken as criticism of Muhammad and his fate was sealed. One evening when he was asleep Salim bin Umaeer pushed a sword in him and killed him.

Ibn Abi Haqqika was another Jew who was killed by Abu Rafa'a reported by Al Bukhari in Fath al bari'e vol 7 page 345. Others who were killed as per this reference were A'Ndeer bin Al Harith, Aqaba bin Abi Mu'eet, Al Huriayth bin Naqeez, Ibn Al Zubaree, Qayes bin A'Nama'an, Ka'ab Bani al Ashraf, and the list goes on and on of those that Muhammad ordered to be killed.

The killing of Theo Van Goth and translators of the Satanic verses along with death threats to Geert Wilders and others are all very much a real part of the silencing of any and all critics of Islam and the quelling of any opposition in modern times.

The enemy cannot be threatened from hundreds of miles away. To threaten him or her, one needs to be in some proximity to him, so immigration solves that problem.

Provoking the Quraish by continued skirmishes and then an assault on their caravans led by Abu Sufyan resulted in the Battle of Bader. In the same way the envelope is pushed and pushed until it can go no further; either the host society gives in or there will be a conflict within the community.

The Muslim immigration and the example of Muhammad

Muhammad set out to finish and complete what he had started in Mecca of the empowerment through intensifying and radicalising his followers, giving his new religion an Arabian colour, arousing them to the enmity of the Jews as a divinely appointed duty to be obeyed (Doctrine of *tamkeen*). Once settled, he and his followers began to consider the first steps of *tamkeen*. This consolidation and empowerment of the community was to see an immediate sharp growth in their numbers resulting in the pacification of the enemies around. So after the first encounter with the Quraish and his victory in the Battle of Bader he had many more join him. From that point on, Muhammad began making plans to fully liquidate the Quraish and all their alliances.

Muhammad set up structures of networks, guards, fighters and introduced *zakat* to finance his wars. He used spoils of war as booty and as windfall of bonuses to heighten the excitement of the new converts. He reduced the Jews to a powerless status, which gave an enormous satisfaction to the Aws and Khazaraj seeing their old enemies humiliated. Muhammad declared those Jews who used to pride themselves as the chosen ones and the children of Allah now as sons of apes and swine.

> Sura 5:60:"Say (O Muhammad to the people of the Scripture): 'Shall I inform you of something worse than that, regarding the recompense from Allah: those (Jews) who incurred the Curse of Allah and His Wrath, those of whom (some) He transformed into monkeys and swine, those who worshipped false deities; such are

worse in rank (on the Day of Resurrection in the Hell-fire), and far more astray from the Right Path (in the life of this world).'"

As the Muslim communities endeavoured to emulate Muhammad individually and corporately, all of their demands were presented first as plausible requests. However, this was done with an aim to undermine the values of the host society, and to have these values slowly but subtly replaced with Islamic values.

HISTORICAL AND MODERN-DAY APPLICATION OF THE IMMIGRATION DOCTRINE — THE PREDICTABILITY OF ISLAMIC BEHAVIOUR PATTERNS

The foregoing has been intended to demonstrate to the reader the intricate pattern that was designed and implemented by Muhammad. Historically, the Immigration Doctrine, which became a central 'Allah-inspired' duty worked very effectively, first in the original immigration by Muhammad, but later on in many crucial instances. Here are some notable examples:

1. The original Muslim immigrants from Mecca to **Abyssinia** (Ethiopia) were empowered by Muhammad to carry the message to that country. Initially they went there because of persecution and sought asylum. Having been granted what we may call today 'political refugee' status, they and their descendents consolidated their position. Islamic sources state that even the Negos, King of Abyssinia, eventually converted to Islam, although this cannot be independently confirmed. The Muslim colony in that country later on spread out to Saharan and sub-Saharan Africa, with a notable penetration of Chad and neighbouring regions. The city of Timbuktu became a major Islamic centre[59]. By the 16th century many parts of Africa were Islamised mostly through immigration and trade[60]. Islamic institutions remained intact during and after

---

[59] See this link about Timbuktu http://www.islamonline.net/servlet/Satellite?c=Article_C& cid=1201957622312&pagename=Zone-English-News/NWELayout

[60] http://www.islamonline.net/English/In_Depth/MuslimAfrica/articles/2005/04/article01.shtml

the colonial era that ended after World War II. Today, Islam is the fastest spreading religion in Africa. Already 12 of the 36 states in Nigeria have adopted *Shariah* law as state law, and are encroaching toward other states to do the same. In all these cases *Hijra* methods are employed carefully. However, when violence is called for, the Muslim militants are ready to act and attack non-Muslim areas, mainly Christian. Hundreds of churches have been burned in Nigeria and other countries. Thus immigration (*Hijra*) and *jihad* are employed as the opportunities develop.

2. The Islamisation of **Malaysia** started only 42 years after the death of Muhammad[61]. The first Umayyad Khalifa Mu'awiya sent emissaries to Malaysia who were then followed by others. We quote here an excerpt from the website at the footnote:

> "After the initial introduction of Islam, the religion was spread by local Muslim scholars or *Ulama* from one district to another. Their normal practice was to open a religious training centre called *pondok* or hut from the small sleeping quarters constructed for the students … after graduating, the pupils would go back to their homeland, often in some remote corner of the country, forming a link in the chain between one *ulama'* and another."

Note here how *tamkeen* and *i'dad* were employed side-by-side to spread Islam involving the promotion of a network of Islamic centres that are carefully controlled by the original *Ulama*. Malaysia became a predominantly Muslim territory in less than 200 years after Muhammad. It was all done by implementing *Hijra* methods and doctrines.

3. The Islamisation of **Indonesia** is a major development for the simple reason that this country is today the largest Muslim-majority state with over 200 Million population 90% of whom are

---

[61] http://www.cyberistan.org/islamic/mmalay.htm

Muslims[62]. The pattern described in the quoted reference follows the *Hijra* doctrine with a lot of supporting details. The authors describe the end result of Islamisation in Southeast Asia as, 'Islamicate', being the end result of full Islamisation, politically, culturally, economically and militarily. It started with migrations from nearby Islamised communities in Malaysia and also some persecuted Muslims from Western China during the 13th and 14th centuries. The key in all the developments consisted of predictable steps:

a. Establishment of a nucleus Islamic community with a mosque, Imams and religious teachers

b. Attracting local communities with the promise of unifying competing tribes, but ending with the Islamised tribal leaders taking full charge of the community politically, and religiously

c. Indoctrinating the young by establishing Islamic schools (*Madrassas*) with an initial focus on the memorisation of the Qur'an, learning Arabic and eventually making Arabic as the local language for trade and all other legal activities based on the *Shariah*

d. Once the nucleus in a small community in an Indonesian island became viable, they would impose *Shariah* law on the rest of the community and would impose the *jizyah* tax on them. Resistance to this is met by force

e. The consolidated Islamised islands would fan out to repeat the same pattern to other islands resulting in the full Islamisation of thousands of island communities in the Indonesian archipelago

f. By the 17th century the major Islamised islands such as Java had developed the full military means to bring Islam to the overwhelming majority of the smaller islands.

---

[62] R. Michael Feener and Anna M. Gade, "Patterns Of Islamization in Indonesia: A Curriculum Unit For Post-Secondary Level Educators," Cornell University Southeast Asia Outreach Program, 1998

RM Feener and AM Gade (see footnote 62) provide a vivid description of all these stages. They also present documentary evidence from the famous Muslim explorer, Ibn Batuta. In one of its conclusions the writers state:

> "Islam also came to the vast Malay Archipelago of Southeast Asia, where a majority of the inhabitants gradually converted and developed unique patterns of Muslim culture, just as other peoples had done in the diverse areas of the Muslim world."

4. Today, of course, we are witnessing the greatest Islamisation efforts ever, especially in **Europe, Canada, USA and Latin America** — all the major bastions of Christianity. Aside from the examples cited earlier about the gradual and innocent-looking approaches to introduce *Shariah* (*hijab*, dietary requirements, special rules for Muslims in the work place and schools, family laws and so on), we have been witnessing the application of *tamkeen* in sensitive institutions:

    (i) Almost every university in the West has a Muslim Student Associated (MSA). The role of the MSA is to create an atmosphere for incoming students whereby they find a 'home away from home.' Many students from Muslim countries come from nominal Islamic backgrounds. Within a short period they are indoctrinated in the tenets of Islam, and soon they become strong proponents and advocates, engaging in interfaith dialogues, and *da'wa* activities. Eventually and in conjunction with local mosques, some students are recruited for more serious action, including violent activities. To do so, however, the community organisers would have applied *i'dad*, so that the means for carrying out violent activities are available and the training associated with such already programmed.

    (ii) Islamic studies at all the major universities have been taken over by outright Islamists or academics with strong Islamic sympathies. This is accomplished by funding chair professorships and research programs. Again, this is part of the *tamkeen* strategy. Basically, today any research paper or MS or PhD thesis is to be compliant with certain guidelines. Is it a surprise that in the academic world there is hardly any effort to carry out such fundamental tasks as the textual analysis of the Qur'an or a proper assessment of violence in Islam? In fact, most of what we see from the academics whose programs are almost 100% financed by Muslim countries are attempts to justify what goes on in the name of Islam, and in fact, to promote Islam to make it more acceptable to the Western mind but without compromising on any of the basic doctrines of Islam. There is now an intellectual shield against doing any critical work on Islam coupled with an effort to spread and promote it through these programs.

5. In the economic sphere, Islamic thinkers realised in the 1960's that there is a possibility for developing a new system of 'Islamic Banking and Finance,' governed almost exclusively by *Shariah* requirement that disallows 'usury.' The term 'usury' was interpreted to forbid any form of interest on loans. Although all Muslim-majority countries have banking systems which deal with interests on loans and deposits, just like any other banking systems around the world, we have been witnessing a sharp rise in 'Islamic banking.' From a practical perspective, the modern designers of Islamic banking products have emulated standard banking with some very important qualifiers. For example, if one wants to get a loan to purchase a car, the Islamic bank would provide the funds for purchasing the car. This is technically not a 'loan' but a form of joint ownership. The fraction of the purchaser's ownership increases as he or she makes monthly installment payments to the bank. The total sum of the instalments is equal to the initial purchase price plus a 'fee' charged by the bank, which is equivalent to the interest that is normally charged. In case of default, the bank keeps the car, i.e. the purchaser has no rights in the car until it is

fully paid for, plus the 'fee.' But this is not the main issue here. The main issue is that all transactions with Islamic banking institutions are required to be 'Islamic *Shariah*-compliant.' This means that:

> "Islamic banking is restricted to Islamically acceptable deals, which exclude those involving alcohol, pork, gambling, etc. Thus ethical investing is the only acceptable form of investment, and moral purchasing is encouraged."[63]

Clearly, as Islamic immigrants are pressured to use Islamic banks, they are now pressing for a wider acceptance of various Islamic financial instruments. Non-Muslims who may find it attractive to use these instruments are basically unaware that they are subscribing to 'Islamic morality' which is a code word for the entire Islamic system, i.e. they are making commitments to a whole ideology within the context of a business transaction. Usually the fine print in Islamic contracts would impose severe penalties for lack of compliance. In short, the non-Muslim investors are being told in subtle terms what Muhammad in 630AD told Emperor Heraclius of Byzantium, "Surrender (code word for becoming a Muslim) and be safe (In Arabic, *Aslem Tislam*)." As of November 2008, the size of the Islamic *Shariah*-compliant financial system has reached 4 Trillion US dollars.

6. In the political sphere immigrants have applied the *Hijra* doctrine in a variety of ways. Through the application of *tamkeen* they have managed to create what can be termed 'open ghettos.' These Islamic ghettos are 'open' in the sense that they prevent anyone from entering but retain their freedom to reach the rest of the society. In this sense, they are ever expanding (note our reference to what happened in Malaysia). The more educated and prosperous Muslim immigrants would fan out of the ghetto, but only to estab-

---

[63] http://en.wikipedia.org/wiki/Islamic_banking#History_of_Islamic_banking

lish links to the host community. These links can be in terms of lobby organisations, think tanks, communication media, interfaith community organisations and so on. The *i'dad* happens more inside the ghetto — whereby the network of mosques and Islamic centres play the role of equipping the indoctrinated groups with the means to carry out various activities, and many cases, violent ones. Political action is aimed at this stage in the Islamisation process at two goals: (1) Silencing any criticism of Islam from Muslims and non-Muslims, and (2) Systematic implementation of *Shariah* law. The supporting processes in the financial and academic sectors would provide the ideological rationale for meeting these goals.

CONCLUSION

Islam is neither a religion nor a faith in a personal way, as defined and understood in the West. It is a whole encompassing political system, garbed in religious outfit, addressing every aspect of the life of its adherents.

So when Muslim immigrants refuse assimilation and despise integration, it is done as a political move expressed religiously. Hence, it would be in the interest of the host society and its national security to examine all requests, from a socio–political angle. For every Islamic doctrine is a political dictate aiming to establish itself by undoing the existing systems to control, rule and dominate in every area.

It must be mandatory for all immigrants and particularly Muslim immigrants to sign an undertaking with built-in punitive charges that they would:

(a) Abide by the law of the land

(b) Do their utmost to be integrated and assimilated with the host society

(c) Regard religion as a personal matter of free will choice

(d) Embrace the equality of genders in all aspects

(e) Regard and treat the discriminatory and violent doctrines and teachings of the *Shariah* as inapplicable and ineffective for today

(f) Accept the equality of all Muslims and non-Muslims

(g) Uphold the separation of state and religion

(h) Value and uphold the right of every individual to choose the religion of his or her choice irrespective of the religion of the next of kin or community they might have belonged to by birth or association of any kind.

APPENDIX A:
ISLAM QUESTION AND ANSWER

In the following pages, we list questions and answers taken mostly from the well-acknowledged Islamic website www.islamQA.com, which is routinely visited by Muslims worldwide seeking answers from some of the leading Islamic scholars (*Ulama*). What is quoted here is in regard to the issues associated with the *Hijra* Doctrine and the related doctrines that we tried to explain. In each section we list the main theme as reported on the website followed by our comment on the particular doctrine this them is related to.

Islam Question & Answer
www.islamQA.com

Note:

Whereas in the main document the authors have, as far as possible, standardised English translation and usage of Arabic words, in this section they have followed the conventions used by the individual writers quoted.

Theme I: When is deliberate ambiguity permissible? If it is in cases of necessity. how do we define necessity?

Our comment: This theme relates to the *darura'* doctrine.

Reader Questions: When is deliberate ambiguity valid? If that is in cases of necessity only, then what is the definition of necessity in this case?

Response by the Islamic authority:

The Arabic word *tawriyah* [translated here as deliberate ambiguity] means to conceal something.

Allaah says (interpretation of the meaning):

"Then Allaah sent a crow who scratched the ground to show him how to hide [*yuwaari*] the dead body of his brother. He (the murderer) said: "Woe to me! Am I not even able to be as this crow and to hide the dead body of my brother?" Then he became one of those who regretted" [al-Maa'idah 5:31]

"O Children of Adam! We have bestowed raiment upon you to cover yourselves (screen your private parts – *yuwaari saw'aatikum*) and as an adornment; and the raiment of righteousness, that is better. Such are among the *Ayaat* (proofs, evidences, verses, lessons, signs, revelations, etc.) of Allaah, that they may remember (i.e. leave falsehood and follow truth)" [al-A'raaf 7:26]

From these words. For example, he says, "I do not have a dirham in my pocket," and that is understood to mean that he does not have any money at all, when what he means is that he does not With regard to the meaning in *sharee'ah* terminology, it refers to someone who says something that may appear to have one meaning to the listener but the speaker intends something different that may be understood to have a dirham but he may have a dinar, for example. This is called ambiguity or dissembling.

Deliberate ambiguity is regarded as a legitimate solution for avoiding difficult situations that a person may find himself in when someone asks him about something, and he does not want to tell the truth on the one hand, and does not want to lie, on the other.

Deliberate ambiguity is permissible if it is necessary or if it serves a *shar'i* interest, but it is not appropriate to do it a great deal so that it becomes a habit, or to use it to gain something wrongfully or to deprive someone of his rights.

Al-Nawawi said:

The scholars said: If that is needed to serve some legitimate shar'i interest that outweighs the concern about misleading the person to whom you are speaking, or it is needed for a reason that cannot be achieved without lying, then there is nothing wrong with using deliberate ambiguity as an acceptable alternative. But if there is no interest to be served and no pressing need, then it is *makrooh*, but is not *haraam*. If it is a means of taking something wrongfully or depriving someone of their rights, then it is *haraam* in that case. This is the guideline in this matter.

Al-Adhkaar, p. 380

Some scholars were of the view that it is *haraam* to resort to deliberate ambiguity if there is no reason or need to do so. This was the view favoured by Shaykh al-Islam Ibn Taymiyah (may Allaah have mercy on him). See al-Ikhtiyaaraat, p. 563.

There are situations in which the Prophet (peace and blessings of Allaah be upon him) taught that we may use deliberate ambiguity, for example: If a man loses his *wudoo'* whilst praying in congregation, what should he do in this embarrassing situation? The answer is that he should place his hand over his nose and leave.

The evidence for that is the report narrated from 'Aa'ishah (may Allaah be pleased with her) who said: The Messenger of Allaah (peace and blessings of Allaah be upon him) said: "If anyone of you breaks his *wudoo'* whilst praying, let him hold his nose and leave." Sunan Abi Dawood, 1114. See also Saheeh Sunan Abi Dawood, 985.

Al-Teebi said: The command to hold his nose is so that it will look as if he has a nosebleed. This is not a lie, rather it is a kind of ambiguity. This concession is granted so that the Shaytaan will not trick him into staying put because of feeling embarrassed in front of people.

Mirqaah al-Mafaateeh Sharh Mishkaat al-Masaabeeh, 3/18

This is a kind of ambiguity that is permitted, so as to avoid any embarrassment and so that whoever sees him leaving will think that he has a nosebleed.

Similarly, if a Muslim faces a difficult situation where he needs to say what is against the truth in order to protect himself or someone who is innocent, or to save himself from serious trouble, is there a way for him to escape the situation without lying or falling into sin?

Yes, there is a legal way and a permissible escape that one can make use of if necessary. It is equivocation or indirectness in speech. Imaam al-Bukhaari (may Allaah have mercy on him) entitled a chapter of his Saheeh: "Indirect speech is a safe way to avoid a lie". (Saheeh al-Bukhaari, Kitaab al-Adab (Book of Manners), chapter 116).

Equivocation means saying something which has a closer meaning that the hearer will understand, but it also has a remote meaning which what is actually meant and is linguistically correct. The condition for this is that whatever is said should not present a truth as falsity and vice versa. The following are examples of such statements used by the salaf and early imaams, and collected by Imaam Ibn al-Qayyim in his book Ighaathat al-Lahfaan:

It was reported about Hammaad (may Allaah have mercy on him), if someone came that he did not want to sit with, he would say as if in pain: "My tooth, my tooth!" Then the boring person whom he did not like would leave him alone.

Imaam Sufyaan Al-Thawri was brought to the khaleefah al-Mahdi, who liked him, but when he wanted to leave, the khaleefah told him he had to stay. Al-Thawri swore that he would come back. He then went out, leaving his shoes at the door. After some time he came back, took his shoes and went away. The khaleefah asked about him, and was told that he had sworn to come back, so he had come back and taken his shoes.

Imaam Ahmad was in his house, and some of his students, including al-Mirwadhi, were with him. Someone came along, asking for al-Mirwadhi from outside the house, but Imaam Ahmad did not want him to go out, so he said: "Al-Mirwadhi is not here, what would he be doing here?" whilst putting his finger in the palm of his other hand, and the person outside could not see what he was doing.

Other examples of equivocation or indirectness in speech include the following:

If someone asks you whether you have seen so-and-so, and you are afraid that if you tell the questioner about him this would lead to harm, you can say "ma ra'aytuhu", meaning that you have not cut his lung, because this is a correct meaning in Arabic ["ma ra'aytuhu" usually means "I have not seen him," but can also mean "I have not cut his lung"]; or you could deny having seen him, referring in your heart to a specific time and place where you have not seen him. If someone asks you to swear an oath that you will never speak to so-and-so, you could say, "Wallaahi lan ukallumahu", meaning that you will not wound him, because "kalam" can also mean "wound" in Arabic [as well as "speech"]. Similarly, if a person is forced to utter words of kufr and is told to deny Allaah, it is permissible for him to say "Kafartu bi'l-laahi", meaning "I denounce the playboy" [which sounds the same as the phrase meaning "I deny Allaah."]

(Ighaathat al-Lahfaan by Ibn al-Qayyim, 1/381 ff., 2/106-107. See also the section on equivocation (ma'aareed) in Al-Adaab al-Shar'iyyah by Ibn Muflih, 1/14).

However, one should be cautious that the use of such statements is restricted only to situations of great difficulty, otherwise: excessive use of it may lead to lying.

One may lose good friends, because they would always be in doubt as to what is meant.

If the person to whom such a statement is given comes to know that the reality was different from what he was told, and he was not aware that the person was engaging in deliberate ambiguity or equivocation, he would consider that person to be a liar. This goes against the principle of protecting one's honour by not giving people cause to doubt one's integrity..

The person who uses such a technique frequently may become proud of his ability to take advantage of people.

End quote. From Madha taf'al fi'l-haalaat al-aatiyah (What to do in the following situations)?

And Allaah knows best.

Theme 2: Is it permissible for a woman to uncover her face in order to seek knowledge?

Our Comment: This is also related to the *darura'* doctrine.

Reader Question: I heard on TV one day that it is permissible for girls or women to uncover their faces in order to seek knowledge. I do not remember which *madhhab* that was, but the speaker said that the Messenger (peace and blessings of Allaah be upon him) said: "The difference of opinion among the *fuqaha'* of my *ummah* is a mercy." Especially since I am finding it difficult to move from being unveiled to wearing *hijab* and *jilbaab*. Please tell me what is right so that I can follow it.

Response by the Islamic authority:

Firstly: The *hadeeth* "The difference of opinion among the *fuqaha'* of my *ummah* is a mercy" is a fabricated *hadeeth*, as it says in Asraar al-Marfoo'ah, 506 and Tanzeeh al-Sharee'ah, 2/402.

Shaykh al-Albaani said of this hadeeth in al-Silsilah al-Da'eefah wa'l-Mawdoo'ah (*hadeeth* no. 57): It has no basis, and the muhaddithoon (scholars of *hadeeth*) tried hard to find an *isnaad* for it but without success.

Al-Manaawi narrated that al-Subki said: It is not known to the muhaddithoon, and I could not find any *isnaad* for it, whether *saheeh*, *da'eef* or *mawdoo'*. This was confirmed by Zakariya al-Ansaari in his commentary on Tafseer al-Baydaawi.

End quote

It is not permissible for a woman to uncover her face in front of non-*mahram* men, except in cases of necessity, such as a medical doctor when no female doctor is available, so long as she is not alone with him (*khulwah*), or when proposing marriage, or when bearing witness in front of a *qaadi* (judge). In the cases mentioned above, it should be limited only to that which is necessary, and no more than that.

A woman's *hijab* and *niqab* do not pose an obstacle to her seeking knowledge. It is not correct to believe that there is a contradiction between covering and seeking knowledge. May Allaah never bless knowledge that is only acquired by means of sin and women neglecting modesty. Women who wear *hijab* and are covered have reached the highest levels of knowledge and have earned degrees and certificates without mixing with men or uncovering their faces, whilst we see many of those who fail to acquire knowledge wearing the minimum of clothing on their bodies. Since when does neglecting modesty bring knowledge and *hijab* prevent it?

Covering the face is obligatory for Muslim women who have reached the age of adolescence. In the answer to question no. 12525 you will find an explanation that the face is *'awrah.*

We have discussed the evidence that it is obligatory to cover the face in the answer to question no. 21134, 21536 and 11774.

The view that it is permissible for women to uncover their faces in order to seek knowledge is not correct.

We ask Allaah to help you to do that which pleases Him, and to reward you greatly for your question and your efforts to learn. Our advice to you is to keep away from dubious places where mixing takes place. We give you the glad tidings from the Prophet (peace and blessings of Allaah be upon him) who said: "Whoever gives up a thing for the sake of Allaah, Allaah will compensate him with something better than it." So seek the help of Allaah and be patient. The first Muslim women gave up their (former) religion, their husbands and their homelands in order to enter Islam, and this move from being uncovered to wearing hijab is insignificant in comparison to what those women did. Be sure that you will find encouragement from your veiled sisters who will make that transition easier for you. Do not pay any attention to the obstacles put in your way by evil and corrupt people, women and men alike, for they do not wish you well and they do not want you to be happy or be rewarded, nor do they know the true path to happiness and reward.

And Allaah knows best.

Theme 3: Ruling on a woman leading men in prayer

Our comment: This is related to *darura'*, whereby although women are not supposed to lead men in prayer for a large number of cases, yet, scholars found ways for women to do so under very special circumstances.

Reader Question: What is the ruling on a woman leading men in Jumu'ah and other prayers?

Firstly:

Allaah has singled out men for some virtues and rulings, and He has singled out women for other virtues and rulings. It is not permissible for any man to wish for that which has been granted to women only, nor is it permissible for any woman to wish for that which has been granted to men. This kind of wishing is tantamount to objecting to the laws and rulings of Allaah.

Allaah says (interpretation of the meaning): "And wish not for the things in which Allaah has made some of you to excel others. For men there is reward for what they have earned, (and likewise) for women there is reward for what they have earned, and ask Allaah of His Bounty. Surely, Allaah is Ever All-Knower of everything" [al-Nisa' 4:32]

al-Sa'di (may Allaah have mercy on him) said: Allaah forbids the believers to wish for that with which Allaah has favoured others, whether that is in things that are possible or things that are impossible. Women should not wish for the things that have been bestowed uniquely upon men, by which Allaah has favoured them over women, and no poor person or person who has shortcomings should merely wish for the position of one who is rich or perfect, because this is the essence of destructive envy (*hasad*)... and because that implies displeasure with the decree of Allaah.

One of the things for which Allaah has singled out men is that the acts of worship which require physical strength, such as jihad, or require a position of leadership such as leading the prayers, etc., are only for men, and women have nothing to do with them.

This is indicated by a great deal of evidence, such as the following:

1 – Allaah says (interpretation of the meaning): "Men are the protectors and maintainers of women, because Allaah has made one of them to excel the other, and because they spend (to support them) from their means" [al-Nisa' 4:34]

al-Shaafa'i said in al-Umm (1/191): If a woman leads men, women and boys in prayer, then the prayer of the women is valid and the prayer of the men and boys is invalid, because Allaah has given men the role of protectors and maintainers of women, and He has not allowed them to be in charge, so it is not permissible for a woman to lead a man in prayer under any circumstances, ever.

Al-Sa'di (may Allaah have mercy on him) said: Men have been favoured over women in numerous ways, such as the fact that positions of leadership and Prophethood are limited to men only, and many acts of worship, such as jihad and leading the Eid prayers and Jumu'ah prayers, are for men only, and Allaah has favoured them with intellect, wisdom, patience and toughness which women do not share.

2 – Allaah says (interpretation of the meaning): "And they (women) have rights (over their husbands as regards living expenses) similar (to those of their husbands) over them (as regards obedience and respect) to what is reasonable, but men have a degree (of responsibility) over them. And Allaah is All-Mighty, All-Wise" [al-Baqarah 2:228]

al-Sa'di (may Allaah have mercy on him) said: "but men have a degree over them" means higher status and leadership, and more rights over them, as Allaah says, "Men are the protectors and maintainers of women". The position of Prophet and judge, leading the prayers and leading the state, and all positions of authority, are restricted to men.

3 – al-Bukhaari (4425) narrated that Abu Bakrah (may Allaah be pleased with him) said: The Messenger of Allaah (peace and blessings of Allaah be upon him) said: "No people will ever succeed who appoint a woman as their leader."

This *hadeeth* indicates that it is not permissible for a woman to hold a position of public authority, and leading the prayers is a position of public authority.

4 – Abu Dawood (576) and Ahmad (5445) narrated that Ibn 'Umar (may Allaah be pleased with him) said: The Messenger of Allaah (peace and blessings of Allaah be upon him) said: "Do not prevent your women from attending the mosques, although their houses are better for them." Classed as saheeh by al-Albaani in Sunan Abi Dawood.

It says in 'Awn al-Ma'bood: "although their houses are better for them" means: their praying in their houses is better for them than their praying in the mosques, if only they knew, but they do not know that, and they ask for permission to go out to the mosques, because they think that the reward for them in the mosque is greater. The reason why their praying at home is better is that there is no danger of *fitnah*. That was confirmed after women began to wear adornments.

5 – Muslim (440) narrated that Abu Hurayrah (may Allaah be pleased with him) said: The Messenger of Allaah (peace and blessings of Allaah be upon him) said: "The best rows for men are those at the front and the worst are those at the back, and the best rows for women are those at the back and the worst are those at the front."

Al-Nawawi said:

The phrase "the rows for men" is to be understood in general terms as meaning that the best of them are those that are at the front, and the worst are those at the back, and that is always the case. As for the rows for women, what is meant in this *hadeeth* is the rows of women who are praying with men. But if women are praying on their own and not with men, then they are like men and the best rows are those at the front and the worst are those at the back. What is meant by the worst rows for both men and women is that they bring less reward, are lower in status and are further removed from what is required by *sharee'ah*. And the best rows are the opposite of that. The virtue of the last row for women who are praying with men is that they are farther away from mixing with men or seeing them or becoming attracted to them when seeing their movements or hearing their words and so on. The first rows are condemned for the opposite of that. And Allaah knows best.

If a woman is enjoined to pray in her house and keep away from men, and the worst rows for women are the front rows, because they are closer to the men, then how can it be befitting for Islam to allow a woman to pray as an imam, leading men in prayer, when it enjoins her to keep away from men?

6 – al-Bukhaari (684) and Muslim (421) narrated from Sahl ibn Sa'd al-Saa'idi that the Messenger of Allaah (peace and blessings of Allaah be upon him) said, "Whoever notices anything amiss during the prayer, let him say *tasbeeh*, for if he does so it will be noticed; and clapping is only for women."

al-Haafiz said: It is as if women are not allowed to say *tasbeeh* because they are enjoined to keep their voices low in prayer at all times, because of the fear of *fitnah*.

If women are forbidden to alert the imam by speaking if he makes a mistake, and should clap instead, so that they will not raise their voice in the presence of men, then how can it be allowed for a woman to lead them in prayer and deliver a *khutbah* to them?

7 – Muslim (658) narrated from Anas ibn Maalik that he prayed behind the Messenger (peace and blessings of Allaah be upon him) and with him was his grandmother and an orphan. He said: The orphan and I stood in a row behind him, and the old woman stood behind us.

Al-Haafiz said: This shows that a woman should not stand in a row with a man. The basic reason is that there is the fear of *fitnah* because of her.

If a woman should stand on her own behind the rows, and not stand in the same row as the men, how can she stand in front of them and lead them in prayer?

It says in 'Awn al-Ma'bood: This indicates that it is not permissible for a woman to lead men in prayer, because if she is not allowed to stand in the same row as them, it is less likely that she should be allowed to stand in front of them.

8 – According to the actions of the Muslims throughout fourteen hundred years, no woman should be allowed to lead men in prayer.

Badaa'i' al-Sanaa'i', 2/289

Whoever goes against this is following a path other than that of the believers. Allaah says (interpretation of the meaning): "And whoever contradicts and opposes the Messenger (Muhammad) after the right path has been shown clearly to him, and follows other than the believers' way, We shall keep him in the path he has chosen, and burn him in Hell — what an evil destination!" [al-Nisa' 4:115]

There follow some comments of the scholars:

It says in al-Mawsoo'ah al-Fiqhiyyah (6/205): In order to lead men in prayers, it is essential that the imam be a male; it is not valid for a woman to lead men in prayers. The *fuqaha'* are unanimously agreed on this matter.

Ibn Hazm said in Maraatib al-Ijmaa', p. 27: They are unanimously agreed that a woman should not lead men in prayer when they know that she is a woman. If they do that then their prayer is invalid, according to scholarly consensus.

It says in al-Muhalla (2/167): It is not permissible for a woman to lead a man or men in prayer. There is no difference of scholarly opinion on this point. Moreover the text states that a woman invalidates a man's prayer if she walks in front of him... The ruling of the Prophet (peace and blessings of Allaah be upon him) is that she should definitely stand behind the man in prayer, and the imam must stand in front of the congregation or with one who is praying with him in the same row... From these texts it may be established that it is definitely invalid for a woman to lead a man or men in prayer.

Al-Nawawi (4/152) said in al-Majmoo (4/152): Our companions are agreed that it is not permissible for an adult man or a boy to pray behind a woman... the prohibition on a woman leading men in prayer applies equally to obligatory prayers, *Taraweeh* and all supererogatory prayers. This is our view and the view of all the scholars from the earlier and later generations – may Allaah have mercy on them. Al-Bayhaqi narrated this from the seven *fuqaha'*, the Taabi'i fuqaha' of Madeenah. It is also the view of Maalik, Abu Haneefah, Sufyaan, Ahmad and Dawood:

Moreover if a woman leads a man or men in prayer, the men's prayer is invalid, but her prayer and the prayer of any women who pray behind her is valid in all prayers, except if she leads them in *Jumu'ah* prayer, in which case there are two views, the most sound of which is that her prayer does not count. The second view is that it does count and it takes the place of *Zuhr*. This is the view of Shaykh Abu Haamid, but it does not amount to anything. And Allaah knows best.

In al-Insaaf (2/265) it says: " A woman's leading a man in prayer is not valid" – This is our view in general – meaning the madhhab of Imam Ahmad – it says in al-Mustaw'ib: This is the correct view.

The Maaliki view concerning this matter is the strictest of all. They do not allow a woman to lead even other women in prayer, and they regard maleness as an essential condition for leading the prayer in all cases. In al-Fawaakih al-Dawaani it says (1/204): Note that there are conditions for leading the prayer to be valid and complete. The conditions of it being valid are thirteen, the first of which is being male; it is not valid for a woman or an effeminate man to lead the prayer. The prayer of the one who prays behind a woman is invalid but not the prayer of the female who led the prayer.

Shaykh Ibn Baaz (may Allaah have mercy on him) was asked about a man who prayed 'Asr behind his wife. He replied: It is not permissible for a woman to lead a man in prayer and his prayer offered behind her is not valid, because of a great deal of evidence to that effect, and the man mentioned must repeat his prayer."

Majmoo' Fataawa Ibn Baaz, 12/130

Secondly:

With regard to the evidence presented by those who refer to the reports which say that the Prophet (peace and blessings of Allaah be upon him) gave Umm Waraqah permission to led her household in prayer (narrated by Abu Dawood, 591), they say that she used to lead the people of her house in prayer, among whom were men and boys.

The scholars have given several answers to that:

1 — The hadeeth is *da'eef* (weak).

Al-Haafiz said in al-Talkhees (p. 121): Its isnaad includes 'Abd al-Rahmaan ibn Khallaad who is unknown.

It says in al-Muntaqa Sharh al-Muwatta': This hadeeth is one to which no attention should be paid.

2 — Even if the *hadeeth* is *saheeh*, what it means is that she used to lead the women of her household in prayer.

3 — That was something that applied only to Umm Waraqah, and it is not prescribed for anyone else.

4 — Some scholars quote it as evidence that a woman may lead a man in prayer, but only in cases of necessity, and what is meant by necessity is when there is no man who can recite al-Faatihah properly. Haashiyat Ibn Qaasim, 2/313

See al-Mughni. 3/33.

Theme 4: Qualities which must be present in the land to which one makes *Hijrah*

Our comment: This is related to the *tamkeen* (empowerment) and *i'dad* (preparation) doctrines.

Reader Question: What are the necessary qualities which must be present in a country for it to be regarded as *daar harb* or *daar kufr* (hostile land or the abode of kufr)?

Every land or region in which the rulers and those in authority uphold the limits set by Allaah and they rule their people in accordance with Islamic *sharee'ah*, and the people are able to carry out what Islam has enjoined upon them, is considered to be *dar islaam* (the abode of Islam). The Muslims in such lands have to obey their rulers with regard to that which is right (*ma'roof*) and be sincere towards them, helping them to take care of the affairs of state and giving them moral and practical support. They should live there, and not go to live anywhere else except to another place which is under Islamic rule where they may be better off. This is like the case of Madeenah after the *Hijrah* of the Prophet (peace and blessings of Allaah be upon him), when the Islamic state was established there, and like Makkah after the Conquest, when the Muslims took power there and it became *daar islaam* after it had been *daar harb* and it had been obligatory for the Muslims there who were able to leave, to migrate from it.

Every country or region in which the rulers and those in authority do not uphold the limits set by Allaah and do not govern those who are under their care by the rules of Islam, and in which the Muslims are not able to establish the rituals of Islam, is *daar kufr* (the abode of *kufr*). This is like Makkah al-Mukarramah before the Conquest, when it was *daar kufr*. The same applies to any land in which the people belong to the religion of Islam, but those who are in authority govern by laws other than those revealed by Allaah, and the Muslims are not able to establish the rituals of their religion. They have to migrate from that place, fleeing so that their religious commitment will not be compromised, to a land which is ruled by Islam and where they will be able to do that which is required of them by *sharee'ah*. Whoever is unable to migrate – men, women or children – will be excused, but Muslims in other lands are obliged to save them and bring them from the *kaafir* lands to the Muslim land. Allaah says (interpretation of the meaning):

"Verily, as for those whom the angels take (in death) while they are wronging themselves (as they stayed among the disbelievers even though emigration was obligatory for them), they (angels) say (to them): "In what (condition) were you?" They reply: "We were weak and oppressed on the earth." They (angels) say: "Was not the earth of Allaah spacious enough for you to emigrate therein?" Such men will find their abode in Hell — what an evil destination! Except the weak ones among men, women and children who cannot devise a plan, nor are they able to direct their way. These are they whom Allaah is likely to forgive, and Allaah is Ever Oft-Pardoning, Oft-Forgiving" [al-Nisaa' 4:97-99]

"And what is wrong with you that you fight not in the Cause of Allaah, and for those weak, ill-treated and oppressed among men, women, and children, whose cry is: "Our Lord! Rescue us from this town whose people are oppressors; and raise for us from You one who will protect, and raise for us from You one who will help." [al-Nisaa' 4:75]

But whoever is able to establish the rituals of Islam within his family and establish evidence against the rulers and people in authority, and bring about reform, making them change their ways, then it is prescribed for him to stay among them, because there is the hope that by staying there he may be able to convey the message and reform them – so long as he is safe from temptation and *fitnah*.

And Allaah is the source of strength. May Allaah bless our Prophet Muhammad.

Fataawaa al-Lajnah al-Daa'imah, 12/51

Theme 5: Should she take off her *hijab* because of the harassment that she is faced with after the London bombings?

Our comment: This is a *darura'* (necessity) related issue.

Reader Question: Following the bombings on July 7th, many Muslim women in Britain were faced with harassment which may lead to killing by extremists in some cases. Is it permissible for a Muslim woman living there in those circumstances to take off her *hijab* so as to avoid possible harassment?

Before issuing a general *fatwa* in such cases it is essential to have a complete picture of the situation and find out whether or not it has reached the degree of necessity which would make it permissible to do a *haraam* deed on which there is consensus that it is *haraam*.

It seems that it has not reached this stage, rather these are the actions of a few fools and extremists, and it is not a general trend in that country. Rather as some of them have said, it is just a few instances of provocation and harassment which can be dealt with without such a serious compromise. Based on that, the Muslims have to ask for their rights to protection, and they should not be blamed for the actions of others, or compromise on practising their religion which is the source of their pride and distinction.

We must remember that *hijab* is an obligation that Allaah has enjoined on the Muslim woman, which is proven in the Qur'aan and the *saheeh Sunnah*, and the *ummah* is agreed upon despite the differences in their *madhhabs* and schools of thought. No *madhhab* has deviated from this view, and no *faqeeh* has gone against it, and this is what the practice of the *ummah* has been throughout the centuries. Allaah says (interpretation of the meaning): "O Prophet! Tell your wives and your daughters and the women of the believers to draw their cloaks (veils) all over their bodies (i.e. screen themselves completely except the eyes or one eye to see the way). That will be better, that they should be known (as free respectable women) so as not to be annoyed. And Allaah is Ever Oft-Forgiving, Most Merciful"

[al-Ahzaab 33:59]

"and to draw their veils all over *Juyoobihinna* (i.e. their bodies, faces, necks and bosoms) and not to reveal their adornment" [al-Noor 24:31]

It is the duty of every Muslim to adhere to the obligations of his religion, and to strive to please his Lord and obey His commands, and no one should force him by any means to give that up.

You would be surprised to see people who advocate freedom and the protection of human rights taking away the freedom of others because of some actions that they had nothing to do with.

With regard to a Muslim woman taking off her *hijab* because of her being faced with harassment, we may sum up this issue in the following points:

It is not permissible for a Muslim woman to stay in a land where she cannot practise her faith openly. Based on that, every Muslim woman who lives there and is not able to practise her faith openly must migrate to a land where she can practice her faith openly with complete freedom.

If she is not able to migrate, then the Muslim woman in such circumstances should stay home, especially if she has a guardian who can look after her and meet her needs, and she should not go out except in cases of necessity, for fear of the *fitnah* (turmoil) to which she may be exposed.

It is not necessary for her to go out to work and study if there is someone who can support her and she can delay her study until the next semester or take a leave of absence from work, until things calm down, because this harassment only happens in the days following an incident, then it soon calms down and things go back to normal.

But if she goes out for some necessary reason and she is afraid that she may face harassment, then she should look at what kind of harassment it is. If it is something that can be put up with, such as swearing or insults, or just hostile looks from some people, this does not mean that it becomes permissible for her to take off her *hijab*, because one can put up with this kind of harassment. It is false to say to a woman: give up your *hijab* because of some words that you hear on the street; rather she should be patient and put up with it. This comes under the heading of testing the faith of the believing woman. Allaah says (interpretation of the meaning):

Do people think that they will be left alone because they say: "We believe," and will not be tested?

3. And We indeed tested those who were before them. And Allaah will certainly make (it) known (the truth of) those who are true, and will certainly make (it) known (the falsehood of) those who are liars, (although Allaah knows all that before putting them to test)" [al-'Ankaboot 29:2-3]

So she should put up with any harassment or mockery that comes for the sake of Allaah, and keep in mind what Allaah has promised of reward to the one who adheres to His religion, as the Prophet (peace and blessings of Allaah be upon him) said: "Ahead of you there is a time of patience when the one who adheres to Islam will have the reward of fifty martyrs among you." Narrated by al-Tabaraani from Ibn Mas'ood and classed as saheeh by al-Albaani in Saheeh al-Jaami'.

• Another means of warding off harassment is not to go out alone, but only in the company of her guardian (*wali*) or as part of a group, so that the foolish will not harass her when she is alone.

• If she is going to be faced with unbearable harassment, such as being beaten or killed or having her honour tarnished, and she has to go out for some necessary reason, then in this case it is permissible for her to reduce her *hijab* to a lesser kind, such as covering the head and neck only. She may give up only as much of her *hijab* as will protect her from being exposed to harm, because necessity should not be exaggerated. Or she may cover herself without the kind of *hijab* that people are used to, so that the Muslim woman will not appear as a target for harassment in the eyes of those people. Among the winter clothing of non-Muslim women there are garments which cover all or most of the parts that are required to be covered by *sharee'ah*.

• If her *hijab* is taken from her by force, then she is being put to trial and she will be rewarded, but she must go back to her proper dress when the problem comes to an end.

Such a fatwa must be issued with caution and in a gradual fashion, according to the situation, so that it will not lead to a loss of Islamic identity in societies that are not conservative.

Theme 6: Should he go back and live in a *kaafir* country?

Our comment: This is related to the entire matter of living in a non-Muslim country and the related duties associated with *Hijra*. It covers several of the issues that we dealt with.

Reader Question: I have been advised by several Muslims who are knowledgeable in Islam against living in a *kaffir* country (America). I am an American/Arab who has lived in America all my life but for a few months now was living in an Arabic country, however things are getting hard for me to continue living here (lack of income, housing, etc.) and am considering going back to America, also another strong reason is that the health care system is better and free for my wife who is ill. Please give me as much a detailed answer from the *hadith* and *quran* as you can as I don't know for sure if I should strive to continue living here or go back to America regarding Islam.

Praise be to Allaah.

The basic principle is that it is *haraam* to settle among the *mushrikeen* and in their land. If Allaah makes it easy for a person to move from such a country to a Muslim country, then he should not prefer that which is inferior [i.e., living in a non-Muslim country] to that which is better [living in a Muslim country] unless he has an excuse which permits him to go back.

We advise you, as others have, not to go and live in a *kaafir* country, unless you are forced to go there temporarily, such as seeking medical treatment that is not readily available in a Muslim country.

Note that whoever gives up a thing for the sake of Allaah, Allaah will compensate him with something better, and that with hardship comes ease, and that whosoever fears Allaah and keeps his duty to Him, He will make a way for him to get out (from every difficulty), and He will provide him from (sources) he never could imagine. You should also note that preserving one's capital is better than taking a risk in the hope of making a profit; the Muslim's capital is his religion, and he should not risk it for the sake of some transient worldly gain.

Shaykh Ibn 'Uthaymeen (may Allaah have mercy on him) issued a detailed *fatwa* concerning the issue of settling in a *kaafir* country, which we will quote here.

Shaykh Ibn 'Uthaymeen said:

Settling in a *kaafir* country poses a great danger to the Muslim's religious commitment, morals, behaviour and etiquette. We and others have seen how many of those who settled there went astray and came back different from when they went; they have come back as evildoers, and some have come back having apostatized from their religion and disbelieving in it and in all other religions – we seek refuge with Allaah – denying it completely and mocking the religion and its people, past and present. Hence we must take measures to guard against that and stipulate conditions which will prevent people from following this path which leads to doom and destruction.

There are two basic conditions which must be met before staying in *kaafir* countries:

The first condition is that the person must be secure in his religious commitment, so that he has enough knowledge, faith and will power to ensure that he will adhere firmly to his religion and beware of deviating or going astray, and that he has an attitude of enmity and hatred of the *kaafirs* and will not befriend them and love them, for befriending them and loving them are things that contradicts faith. Allaah says (interpretation of the meaning):

"You (O Muhammad) will not find any people who believe in Allaah and the Last Day, making friendship with those who oppose

Allaah and His Messenger (Muhammad), even though they were their fathers or their sons or their brothers or their kindred (people)" [al-Mujaadilah 58:22]

And He says (interpretation of the meaning):

"O you who believe! Take not the Jews and the Christians as Awliyaa' (friends, protectors, helpers), they are but *Awliyaa'* of each other. And if any amongst you takes them (as *Awliyaa'*), then surely, he is one of them. Verily, Allaah guides not those people who are the *Zaalimoon* (polytheists and wrongdoers and unjust).

And you see those in whose hearts there is a disease (of hypocrisy), they hurry to their friendship, saying: 'We fear lest some misfortune of a disaster may befall us.' Perhaps Allaah may bring a victory or a decision according to His Will. Then they will become regretful for what they have been keeping as a secret in themselves" [al-Maa'idah 5:51, 52]

And it was narrated in al-Saheeh that the Prophet (peace and blessings of Allaah be upon him) said: "Whoever loves a people is one of them" and that "A man will be with the one whom he loves."

Loving the enemies of Allaah is one of the most serious dangers for the Muslim, because loving them implies that one agrees with them and follows them, or at the very least that one does not denounce them, hence the Prophet (peace and blessings of Allaah be upon him) said, "Whoever loves a people is one of them."

The second condition is that he should be able to practise his religion openly, so that he can observe the rituals of Islam with no impediment. So he will not be prevented from establishing regular prayer, and praying *Jumu'ah* and offering prayers in congregation if there are others there with whom he can pray in congregation and pray *Jumu'ah*; and he will not be prevented from paying *zakaah*, fasting, performing *Hajj* and doing other rituals of Islam. If he will not be able to do these, then it is not permissible to stay there because it becomes obligatory to migrate (*hijrah*) in that case.

Shaykh Ibn 'Uthaymeen said – explaining the categories of people who settle in non-Muslim lands:

The fourth category includes those who stay for an individual, permissible need, such as doing business or receiving medical treatment. It is permissible for them to stay as long as they need to. The scholars (may Allaah have mercy on them) have stated that it is permissible to go to kaafir countries in order to do business, and they narrated that some of the Sahaabah (may Allaah be pleased with them) had done that.

The Shaykh said – at the end of the *fatwa*:

How can the believer be content to live in the land of the *kuffaar* where the rituals of kufr are proclaimed openly and rule belongs to someone other than Allaah and His Messenger, seeing that with his own eyes, hearing that with his own ears and approving of it, and even starting to feel that he belongs there and living there with his wife and children, and feeling as comfortable there as he does in the Muslim lands, even though he and his wife and children are in such great danger and their religious commitment and morals are in such peril?

Majmoo' Fataawa al-Shaykh Ibn 'Uthyameen, Fatwa no. 388.

See also the answer to question no. <u>14235</u> and <u>3225</u>.

Theme 7: Staying in a *kaafir* country where there is no community or a mosque

Our comment: This is again related to the *Hijra* doctrine, in general, and touches on the related doctrine of "Allegiance and Rejection" (*Al-Walaa' we Al-Baraa'*)

Reader Question: If a Muslim is able to practice his religion openly in a *kaafir* country where he is staying for work, but there is no mosque or (Muslim) community, is he sinning thereby?

Praise be to Allaah.

Firstly:

The evidence indicates that it is *haraam* to settle among the *mushrikeen*, and it is obligatory to migrate from the *kaafir* country to a Muslim country if one is able to do that. Allaah says (interpretation of the meaning):

"Verily, as for those whom the angels take (in death) while they are wronging themselves (as they stayed among the disbelievers even though emigration was obligatory for them), they (angels) say (to them): "In what (condition) were you?" They reply: "We were weak and oppressed on the earth." They (angels) say: "Was not the earth of Allaah spacious enough for you to emigrate therein?" Such men will find their abode in Hell — what an evil destination!" [al-Nisa' 4:97].

The Prophet (peace and blessings of Allaah be upon him) said: "I have nothing to do with any Muslim who settles among the *mushrikeen*." Narrated by Abu Dawood (2645) and classed as *saheeh* by al-Albaani in Saheeh Abi Dawood.

This is the general basic principle: otherwise it is permissible to go to those countries in cases of need, such as to do business, study and so on, so long as one is able to practise Islam openly.

But if it is not possible to practise Islam openly, then it is *haraam* to remain there, and one must migrate from there if possible.

See also the answer to question no. <u>13363</u>.

Secondly:

What is meant by practising Islam openly is proclaiming *Tawheed*, and disavowing *shirk*, and establishing the symbols of Islam without fear. Shaykh Muhammad ibn Ibraaheem Aal al-Shaykh (may Allaah have mercy on him) was asked: Please tell us of the meaning of the *hadeeths*: "Whoever lives with a *mushrik* and mixes with him is like him" and "I have nothing to do with any Muslim who settles among the *mushrikeen*."

He replied:

"Whoever lives with a *mushrik* and mixes with him is like him" and "I have nothing to do with any Muslim who settles among the *mushrikeen*." These two *hadeeths* contain a stern warning and emphatically forbid living with the *mushrikeen* and mixing with them. They also indicate that it is obligatory to migrate from the land of shirk to the land of Islam. This applies to the one who is not able to practise his religion openly. As for the one who is able to practise his religion openly, he is not obliged to migrate, rather it is *mustahabb* in his case, but it may not be *mustahabb* if his remaining among them serves a religious purpose such as calling them to *Tawheed* and the *Sunnah*, and warning them against *shirk* and *bid'ah* in addition to being able to practise his religion openly.

Practising the religion openly does not only refer to praying and minor issues of religion and avoiding *haraam* things such as *riba*, *zina* and so on. Rather practising the religion openly means proclaiming *Tawheed* and disavowing the ways of the *mushrikeen*, such as associating others with Allaah in worship and other kinds of *kufr* and misguidance. End quote from Fataawa al-Shaykh Muhammad ibn Ibraaheem (1/77).

Shaykh Saalih al-Fawzaan (may Allaah preserve him) was asked: What is the ruling on one who fears the aggression of the *kuffaar* and *mushrikeen*, and shows approval of some of their evil actions for fear of them, and not because he agrees with or approves of what they do? He replied: It is not permissible for the Muslim to show approval of the *kuffaar* at the expense of his religious commitment, or to agree with their actions and deeds, because their actions may be *kufr*, shirk and major sins, so it is not permissible for the Muslim to agree with what they do or to join them in that of his own accord, rather what he must do is to practise his religion openly.

And it is not permissible for him to live with the *kuffaar* and stay in their land unless he is able to practise his religion openly, such as enjoining what is good and forbidding what is evil, and calling to the way of Allaah, and that is what is meant by practising Islam openly. If he cannot do that, then he must migrate to the Muslim lands from the *kaafir* land, and not stay there at the expense of his religious commitment and belief. End quote from al-Muntaqa (1/254).

Practicing one's religion openly in this manner is not usually possible for the one who lives alone in these countries, or with a small community of Muslims.

Even if we assume that you are able to practice your religion openly, then staying isolated from the Muslims obviously has its bad effects on you, your family and children. It is known that there are generations of Muslims who have lost their religion, language and values because of staying in those countries, where you do not hear the *adhaan*, attend the prayers in congregation or see the believers, and *kufr* surrounds them on all sides and evils are common and are assailing these Muslim communities from all directions.

Hence we advise you to flee for the sake of your religion and to protect yourself and those who are with you, and move to a Muslim country or to a place where there are a lot of Muslims, and you can pray *Jumu'ah* and prayers in congregation with them, and broadcast the *adhaan* openly, and manifest the symbols of Islam.

We present to you advice written by Shaykh Ibn Baaz (may Allaah have mercy on him) that is appropriate to this topic. He said in a letter addressed to a Muslim who was living in Italy:

With regard to your letter in which you say that you are a young Muslim man living in Italy and that there are many young Muslim men there and that most of them responded to the crusaders' wishes by keeping far away from the religion of Islam and its noble teachings, so most of them do not pray and they have bad morals and do evil deeds which they regard as permissible, and other things that you mention in your letter…

I advise you that living in a land in which *shirk* and *kufr*, and Christianity and other religions of *kufr* are prevalent, is not permissible, whether you are staying there for work, business, study or some other purpose, because Allaah says (interpretation of the meaning):

"Verily, as for those whom the angels take (in death) while they are wronging themselves (as they stayed among the disbelievers even though emigration was obligatory for them), they (angels) say (to them): 'In what (condition) were you?' They reply: 'We were weak and oppressed on the earth.' They (angels) say: 'Was not the earth of Allaah spacious enough for you to emigrate therein?' Such men will find their abode in Hell — what an evil destination!

98. Except the weak ones among men, women and children who cannot devise a plan, nor are they able to direct their way.

99. These are they whom Allaah is likely to forgive them, and Allaah is Ever Oft-Pardoning, Oft-Forgiving"

[al-Nisa' 4:97-99]

And because the Prophet (peace and blessings of Allaah be upon him) said: "I have nothing to do with any Muslim who settles among the *mushrikeen*."

This settling among the *kuffaar* is not done by one who knows the real meaning of Islam and faith, or who knows what Allaah has enjoined upon the Muslims, or who is pleased with Allaah as his Lord, Islam as his religion, and Muhammad (peace and blessings of Allaah be upon him) as his Prophet and Messenger.

Being pleased and content with that means loving Allaah, giving precedence to seeking His pleasure, being very concerned about following His religion and keeping company with His close friends, which means that one must completely disavow and keep far away from the *kaafirs* and their lands. Rather faith as defined in the Qur'aan and *Sunnah* cannot coexist with these evils. It is narrated in a *saheeh* report from Jareer ibn 'Abd-Allaah al-Bajali (may Allaah be pleased with him) that he said: O Messenger of Allaah, accept my oath of allegiance and stipulate conditions. The Messenger of Allaah (peace and blessings of Allaah be upon him) said: "Worship Allaah, establish regular prayer, pay *zakaah*, be sincere towards the Muslims and keep away from the *mushrikeen*." Narrated by Abu 'Abd al-Rahmaan al-Nasaa'i. It is also narrated in a *saheeh* report that the Messenger of Allaah (peace and blessings of Allaah be upon him) said: "I have nothing to do with any Muslim who settles among the *mushrikeen*." And he (peace and blessings of Allaah be upon him) said: "Allaah will not accept any deed from a *mushrik* after he becomes Muslim until he leaves the *mushrikeen*."

The scholars have clearly stated that this is not allowed, and have warned against it, and stated that it is obligatory to migrate if one is able, except for a man who has knowledge and insight, and goes there to call people to Allaah and bring people forth from darkness into light, and explain the teachings of Islam to them. A verse in Soorat al-Tawbah – (interpretation of the meaning):

"Say: If your fathers, your sons, your brothers, your wives, your kindred, the wealth that you have gained, the commerce in which you fear a decline, and the dwellings in which you delight are dearer to you than Allaah and His Messenger, and striving hard and fighting in His Cause, then wait until Allaah brings about His Decision (torment). And Allaah guides not the people who are Al-Faasiqoon (the rebellious, disobedient to Allaah)" [al-Tawbah 9:24] – indicates that seeking worldly gains is not a legitimate shar'i excuse, rather the one who does that is a *faasiq* (rebellious evildoer) who is subject to the warning of not being guided if these matters, or some of them, are dearer to him than Allaah and His Messenger, and jihad for the sake of Allaah. What good can there be in seeing *shirk* and other evils and keeping quiet about them, or even doing them, as has happened to some of those whom you mentioned who are supposedly Muslim?

If the Muslim who settles there claims that he has some worldly aims such as study, business or work, that is even worse.

In the Book of Allaah there is a stern warning against merely failing to migrate (*hijrah*), as in the verses of Soorat al-Nisa' quoted above, where Allaah says (interpretation of the meaning): "Verily, as for those whom the angels take (in death) while they are wronging themselves". So how about the one who travels to a *kaafir* land and agrees to settle there? As you mentioned, the scholars (may Allaah have mercy on them) forbade settling and going to a land where the Muslim will not be able to practise his religion openly. The one who are there for study, business or work come under the same ruling as the one who settles there, if they are not able to practise their religion openly and they are able to migrate.

As for the claim of some of them that they hate them and despise them, yet they are settling in their land, that is not sufficient, rather it is *haraam* to travel and settle there for many reasons, including the following:

1 – It is not possible to practise the religion openly in a way that means one has discharged one's duties fully.

2 – The texts and clear statements of the scholars (may Allaah have mercy on them) indicate that if a person does not know his religion with its evidence and proof, and he is not able to defend it and ward off the specious arguments of the *kaafirs*, it is not permissible for him to travel to their land.

3 – One of the conditions of it being permissible to travel to their land is that one should be safe from the *fitnah* of their power, control, specious arguments and attractions, and be safe from imitating them or being influenced by their actions.

4 – Blocking the means that may lead to *shirk* is one of the most important principles of Islam. Undoubtedly what you mention in your letter about things that happen with Muslim youth who settle in these

lands is the result of their staying in the land of *kufr*. They should be steadfast in adhering to their religion, practising it openly, following its commands, heeding its prohibitions, and calling others to it, until they are able to migrate from the land of shirk to a Muslim land.

Allaah is the One Whom we ask to set straight all your affairs and to bless you with understanding of His religion and make you steadfast in following it. May He help us and you and all the Muslims to do all that He loves and that pleases Him, and to protect us and you and all the Muslims against things that may lead us astray and against the tricks of the *shaytaan*. May He help us to do all that is good, and support His religion, and make His word supreme, and reform the leaders of the Muslims and bless them with understanding of His religion, and help them to rule according to the *sharee'ah* of Allaah in their lands, and refer to it for judgement, and be content with it and beware of that which goes against it, for He is able to do that. Peace be upon you and the Mercy of Allaah and His blessings.

End quote from Majmoo' Fataawa al-Shaykh Ibn Baaz (9/403).

We ask Allaah to guide you, make things easy for you and help you to find that which is good wherever it may be.

And Allaah knows best.

Theme 8: Official fatwa (in Arabic) regarding *tamkeen* and *i'dad* (empowerment and preparation) under immigration

Our comment: This is a key modern-day *fatwa* (Islamic legal ruling) on the issues of preparedness and empowerment in *Hijra*. It focuses on quotations from the Qur'an and *Hadith* on this major issue. Following is a full translation by the authors. The Arabic original from www.islamweb.net is provided verbatim.

Question: Respected Sheikh, I would like you to elaborate on some of the *Hadiths* or Qur'anic *Aya's* (verses) that point to the reasons for the victory of Muslims in their military campaigns.

Fatwa title: Conditions for victory (Nasr) and empowerment (Tamkeen) for all Muslims.

Fatwa No: 27216

Date: 6-Zhul-Qi'da-1423 Hijri.

Text of the Fatwa following the normal praises to Allah, Muhammad and his companions:

The Holy Qur'an contains full explanations on the conditions for victory and empowerment (*Nasr* and *Tamkeen*) to all Muslims as per Sura 24:55

Allâh has promised those among you who believe, and do righteous good deeds, that He will certainly grant them succession to (the present rulers) in the earth, as He granted it to those before them, and that He will grant them the authority to practise their religion, that which He has chosen for them (i.e. Islâm). And He will surely give them in exchange a safe security after their fear (provided) they (believers) worship Me and do not associate anything (in worship) with Me. But whoever disbelieved after this, they are the *Fâsiqûn* (rebellious, disobedient to Allâh).

And Sura 22:41

Those (Muslim rulers) who, if We give them power in the land, (they) order for Iqamat-as-Salât. [i.e. to perform the five compulsory congregational *Salât* (prayers) (the males in mosques)], to pay the *Zakât* and they enjoin Al-Ma'rûf (i.e. Islâmic Monotheism and all that Islâm orders one to do), and forbid Al-Munkar (i.e. disbelief, polytheism and all that Islâm has forbidden) [i.e. they make the Qur'ân as the law of their country in all the spheres of life]. And with Allâh rests the end of (all) matters (of creatures).

Hence, the rules for Empowerment (*Tamkeen*) as per the first *Sura* are:

1. Complete submissive belief in Islam in all of its meanings and pillars
2. Good works
3. Realization of slavery to Allah
4. Fighting of "Shirk" (Polytheistic belief including Christianity) and washing one's hands from it and all who believe in it.
5. Carrying out Islamic ceremonial prayers (5 time per day)
6. Payment of Islamic tax called "Zakat"
7. Obedience to the Messenger
8. Commanding virtue (*Ma'roof*) and prohibition of vice (*Munkar*){virtue and vice are defined Islamically which is radically different from the humane concept of the West}

As for the material victory causes we note the following:

- *I'dad* (Preparedness in numbers and means) as per Sura 8:60

And make ready against them all you can of power, including steeds of war (tanks, planes, missiles, artillery, etc.) to threaten the enemy of Allâh and your enemy, and others besides whom, you may not know but whom Allâh does know. And whatever you shall spend in the Cause of Allâh shall be repaid unto you, and you shall not be treated unjustly.

The Messenger implemented all of what is stated to the fullest extent and the minutest details in all stages of his missions (*Da'wa's*) and military campaigns. In the *Hijra* (his migration from Mecca to Medina) he accounted for every details, he arranged for the route and the guides, the companion, the places he and his companions would hide and used caution and secrecy. He applied this to all his military campaigns like Badr, Uhud, the Ahzab and others.

Other causes of victory include,

• The religious preparedness (*Rabbaniah*) of those individuals who have taken upon themselves the tasks of spreading the "*Deen*" (i.e. Islamic system) and (military) *Jihad*, for this is exactly what the Messenger used for his own personal preparedness (*I'dad*) from the outset of his call, for he has been very careful to prepare his companions along the religious lines quietly, gradually and in all secrecy. Sura 62:2 states,

He it is Who sent among the unlettered ones a Messenger (Muhammad SAW) from among themselves, reciting to them His Verses, purifying them (from the filth of disbelief and polytheism), and teaching them the Book (this Qur'ân, Islâmic laws and Islâmic jurisprudence) and Al-Hikmah (As-*Sunnah*: legal ways, orders, acts of worship, etc. of Prophet Muhammad SAW). And verily, they had been before in mainfest error;

And Sura 18:28 states,

And keep yourself (O Muhammad SAW) patiently with those who call on their Lord (i.e. your companions who remember their Lord with glorification, praising in prayers, etc., and other righteous deeds, etc.) morning and afternoon, seeking His Face, and let not your eyes overlook them, desiring the pomp and glitter of the life of the world; and obey not him whose heart We have made heedless of Our Remembrance, one who follows his own lusts and whose affair (deeds) has been lost.

Also, the other causes of victory are fighting division and supporting unity, as per Sura 3:103.

And hold fast, all of you together, to the Rope of Allâh (i.e. this Qur'ân), and be not divided among yourselves, and remember Allâh's Favour on you, for you were enemies one to another but He joined your hearts together, so that, by His Grace, you became brethren (in Islâmic Faith), and you were on the brink of a pit of Fire, and He saved you from it. Thus Allâh makes His Ayât (proofs, evidences, verses, lessons, signs, revelations, etc.,) clear to you, that you may be guided.

Another cause of victory is careful planning as evidenced in all the Messenger's actions in the *Hijra*, military campaigns and others.

The reader is referred to the book by Ali Sallabi, "The Jurisprudence of Islamic Preparedness (*Tamkeen*)."

End of Fatwa 27216

In Fatwa 68173, the readers asks the question about the meaning of "Man's succession to the earth."

The response quoted Suras 24:55 and 22:41 as per the previous *Fatwa* and explained that "succession to the earth is to have control of all its resources and all the people living in it." Furthermore, "Allah had promised those who follow Islam, spiritually and materially, to be in ownership of the earth and full control of all who live in it."

The reader is further advised to read other Fatwa's on the same issue: **10091** //**27216** //**14678** //**40112**

فتاوى إسلام ويب

عنوان الفتوى	: شروط النصر والتمكين للمسلمين
رقم الفتوى	: 27216
تاريخ الفتوى	: 06 ذو القعدة 1423

السؤال: فضيلة الشيخ أريد منك أن تستخرج لي بعض الأحاديث النبوية الشريفة أو الآيات القرآنية التي تدل على سبب انتصار المسلمين في غزواتهم.

الفتوى: الحمد لله والصلاة والسلام على رسول الله وعلى آله وصحبه أما بعد:

ففي القرآن الكريم بيان شروط النصر والتمكين للمسلمين، وذلك في قوله تعالى: وَعَدَ اللَّهُ الَّذِينَ آمَنُوا مِنْكُمْ وَعَمِلُوا الصَّالِحَاتِ لَيَسْتَخْلِفَنَّهُمْ فِي الْأَرْضِ كَمَا اسْتَخْلَفَ الَّذِينَ مِنْ قَبْلِهِمْ وَلَيُمَكِّنَنَّ لَهُمْ دِينَهُمُ الَّذِي ارْتَضَى لَهُمْ وَلَيُبَدِّلَنَّهُمْ مِنْ بَعْدِ خَوْفِهِمْ أَمْناً يَعْبُدُونَنِي لَا يُشْرِكُونَ بِي شَيْئاً وَمَنْ كَفَرَ بَعْدَ ذَلِكَ فَأُولَئِكَ هُمُ الْفَاسِقُونَ [النور:55].

وقوله تعالى: الَّذِينَ إِنْ مَكَّنَّاهُمْ فِي الْأَرْضِ أَقَامُوا الصَّلَاةَ وَآتَوُا الزَّكَاةَ وَأَمَرُوا بِالْمَعْرُوفِ وَنَهَوْا عَنِ الْمُنْكَرِ وَلِلَّهِ عَاقِبَةُ الْأُمُورِ [الحج:41].

فشروط التمكين في الآية الأولى هي:

1- الإيمان بكل معانيه وبكافة أركانه.
2- العمل الصالح.
3- تحقيق العبودية لله تعالى.
4- محاربة الشرك والبراءة منه ومن أهله.

وبينت الآية الثانية لوازم استمرار التمكين فجاء فيها:

1- إقامة الصلاة.
2- إيتاء الزكاة.
3- طاعة الرسول.
4- الأمر بالمعروف والنهي عن المنكر.

ومن أسباب النصر المادية:

- الإعداد، كما قال الله تعالى: وَأَعِدُّوا لَهُمْ مَا اسْتَطَعْتُمْ مِنْ قُوَّةٍ وَمِنْ رِبَاطِ الْخَيْلِ تُرْهِبُونَ بِهِ عَدُوَّ اللَّهِ وَعَدُوَّكُمْ [الأنفال:60].

ولقد طبق الرسول صلى الله عليه وسلم هذا الأمر بكل حذافيره في كل مراحل دعوته وفي جميع غزواته، ففي الهجرة -مثلاً- لم يترك الرسول صلى الله عليه وسلم أمراً من الأمور إلا أعد له عدته وحسب حسابه، فقد أعد الرواحل والدليل واختار الرفيق والمكان الذي سيتوارى فيه هو وصاحبه، واستخدم الحذر والكتمان.

وكذلك الأمر بالنسبة لغزواته بدر وأحد والأحزاب، وغيرها.

ومن أسباب النصر:

إعداد الأفراد الربانيين الذين يأخذون على عاتقهم إقامة الدين والجهاد، وهذا ما فعله الرسول صلى الله عليه وسلم منذ اليوم الأول من بعثته، فحرص صلى الله عليه وسلم على إعداد أصحابه إعداداً ربانياً في هدوء وتدرج وسرية، قال الله تعالى: هُوَ الَّذِي بَعَثَ فِي الْأُمِّيِّينَ رَسُولًا مِنْهُمْ يَتْلُو عَلَيْهِمْ آيَاتِهِ وَيُزَكِّيهِمْ وَيُعَلِّمُهُمُ الْكِتَابَ وَالْحِكْمَةَ [الجمعة:2].

وقال تعالى: وَاصْبِرْ نَفْسَكَ مَعَ الَّذِينَ يَدْعُونَ رَبَّهُمْ بِالْغَدَاةِ وَالْعَشِيِّ [الكهف:28].

ومن أسباب النصر: محاربة أسباب الفرقة والأخذ بأصول الوحدة، وفي هذا يقول الله تعالى: وَاعْتَصِمُوا بِحَبْلِ اللَّهِ جَمِيعًا وَلَا تَفَرَّقُوا [آل عمران:103].

ومن أسباب النصر المادية التخطيط.. وهذا واضح جداً في حياة الرسول صلى الله عليه وسلم كما في الهجرة، والغزوات وغيرها.
وننصح السائل الرجوع إلى كتاب فقه التمكين للدكتور على الصلابي ففيه الكفاية. والله أعلم.

<u>المفتـي: مركز الفتوى</u>

www.islamweb.net

فتاوى إسلام ويب

: معنى الاستخلاف في الأرض وكيف نحققه	عنوان الفتوى
: 68173	رقم الفتوى
: 13 رمضان 1426	تاريخ الفتوى

السؤال: ما معنى الاستخلاف في الأرض ؟

الفتوى:

الحمد لله والصلاة والسلام على رسول الله وعلى أله وصحبه، أما بعد:

فإن الاستخلاف في الأرض هو التمكين فيها والملك لها والقيادة والسيادة لمن عليها .

وقد وعد الله تعالى عباده المؤمنين بالاستخلاف والتمكين في الأرض فيها إذا حصلوا حقيقة الإيمان ومقتضياته ، وأخذوا بأسباب التمكين المادية والمعنوية . فقال تعالى : وَعَدَ اللَّهُ الَّذِينَ آمَنُوا مِنكُمْ وَعَمِلُوا الصَّالِحَاتِ لَيَسْتَخْلِفَنَّهُمْ فِي الْأَرْضِ كَمَا اسْتَخْلَفَ الَّذِينَ مِن قَبْلِهِمْ وَلَيُمَكِّنَنَّ لَهُمْ دِينَهُمُ الَّذِي ارْتَضَى لَهُمْ وَلَيُبَدِّلَنَّهُم مِّن بَعْدِ خَوْفِهِمْ أَمْنًا يَعْبُدُونَنِي لَا يُشْرِكُونَ بِي شَيْئًا {النور: 55} وقال تعالى: الَّذِينَ إِن مَّكَّنَّاهُمْ فِي الْأَرْضِ أَقَامُوا الصَّلَاةَ وَآتَوُا الزَّكَاةَ وَأَمَرُوا بِالْمَعْرُوفِ وَنَهَوْا عَنِ الْمُنكَرِ وَلِلَّهِ عَاقِبَةُ الْأُمُورِ {الحج: 41} إلى غير ذلك من الآيات.

ولمزيد من الفائدة والتفصيل نرجو الاطلاع على الفتاوى التالية أرقامها :
10091 //27216 //14678 //40112 .

والله أعلم .

المفتـي: مركز الفتوى

Theme 9: Links to rulings associated with the topic of "residency in foreign, non-Islamic countries"

Our comment: In what follows we discover a wealth of rulings associated with most of the doctrines described in the text.

http://islamweb.net/pls/iweb/fatwa.showSingleFatwa?FatwaId=714

لا تجوز الإقامة ببلاد الكفار إلا لضرورة أو مصلحة راجحة

(It is not permissible to reside in the land of the infidels except for reasons of necessity or profitable gain)

http://islamweb.net/pls/iweb/fatwa.showSingleFatwa?FatwaId=1204

لا يصح طلب جنسية دولة كافرة إلا لضرورة

(It is not correct to become a citizen of an apostate country except for reasons of necessity, *Darura'*)

http://63.175.194.25/index.php?ln=ara&ds=qa&lv=browse&QR=14235&dgn=3

حكم التجنّس بالجنسية الأوربية للمسلم ؟

(Ruling regarding becoming European citizens for Muslims)

http://islamweb.net/pls/iweb/fatwa.showSingleFatwa?FatwaId=1818

لا يجوز السفر إلى بلاد الكفر لقصد التنزه

(It is not recommended that a Muslim travels to an Apostate land for sightseeing and vacation)

http://islamweb.net/pls/iweb/fatwa.showSingleFatwa?FatwaId=1620

إن استطعت إكمال الدراسة في بلدك فهو أفضل

(If possible, it's preferred to complete your studies in your (Muslim) country)

http://islamweb.net/pls/iweb/fatwa.showSingleFatwa?FatwaId=2007

لا تجوز الهجرة من بلاد المسلمين إلى بلاد غير المسلمين إلا في حال الضرورة

(It is not permitted to emigrate from a Muslim country and a non-Muslim one except for *Darura'* (necessity))

http://islamweb.net/pls/iweb/fatwa.showSingleFatwa?FatwaId=7517

دار الإسلام ودار الحرب

(Abode of Islam and Abode of War)

http://islamweb.net/pls/iweb/fatwa.showSingleFatwa?FatwaId=3732

حكم التجنس والإقامة في دولة كافرة والانخراط في جيشها

(Ruling regarding residency and change of citizenship in an Apostate country and enrolment in its army)

http://islamweb.net/pls/iweb/fatwa.showSingleFatwa?FatwaId=3562

حكم الارتحال عن بلد مسلم

(Ruling on departure from a Muslim country)

http://islamweb.net/pls/iweb/fatwa.showSingleFatwa?FatwaId=5045

تجوز الإقامة في بلاد الكفار إذا كانت لغرض الدعوة

(It is permitted to reside in Apostate lands for *Da'wa* purposes)

http://islamweb.net/pls/iweb/fatwa.showSingleFatwa?FatwaId=6341

من يدرس ويقيم في أماكن مختلطة كيف يحفظ صيامه ؟

(How can a Muslim living in pluralistic society study, live and maintain his fast (*Sawm*))

http://islamweb.net/pls/iweb/fatwa.showSingleFatwa?FatwaId=25591

حكم إقامة الفتاة في سكن جامعي في دولة كافرة

(Rule regarding residence of a young Muslim woman at a university in an Apostate land)

http://islamweb.net/pls/iweb/fatwa.showSingleFatwa?FatwaId=12716

حكم السفر لبلاد الكفر لأجل الزواج

(Ruling regarding travel to Apostate lands for purposes of getting married)

http://islamweb.net/pls/iweb/fatwa.showSingleFatwa?FatwaId=16686

الهجرة على ثلاثة أضرب

(*Hijra* times three!)

http://islamweb.net/pls/iweb/fatwa.showSingleFatwa?FatwaId=15708

شروط جواز إعانة مريد الهجرة إلى بلاد الكفر

(Rulings for assisting a person desiring *Hijra* to Apostate lands)

http://islamweb.net/pls/iweb/fatwa.showSingleFatwa?FatwaId=15784

الإقامة في بلاد الكفر لأجل الدعوة جهاد

(Residence in Apostate lands for the *Jihad* call (*Da'wa*))

http://islamweb.net/pls/iweb/fatwa.showSingleFatwa?FatwaId=17601

قد توجد حالات تجعل السكن في بلاد الكفر أفضل

(There may be situations whereby living in Apostate lands is preferred) http://islamweb.net/pls/iweb/fatwa.showSingleFatwa?FatwaId=18886

نوعية الضرورة تحدد جواز الحلف لأخذ الجنسية من عدمه

(Kinds of *Darura'* (necessity) in "oaths" to obtain citizenship)

http://islamweb.net/pls/iweb/fatwa.showSingleFatwa?FatwaId=18462

كيف يحتاط المسلم لدينه في بلاد الكفر

(What precautions can a Muslim carry out to protect his Islam in the Apostate lands)

http://islamweb.net/pls/iweb/fatwa.showSingleFatwa?FatwaId=20063

هل ترخص الهجرة لديار الكفر لتحسين المعيشة

(Is *Hijra* to Apostate lands permissible for purposes of improving living conditions?)

http://islamweb.net/pls/iweb/fatwa.showSingleFatwa?FatwaId=20969

رغبة الأب في دراسة ابنه في ديار الكفر...نظرة شرعية

(A *Shariah* jurisprudence look at the desire of a father to send his son to study in Apostate lands)

http://islamweb.net/pls/iweb/fatwa.showSingleFatwa?FatwaId=21567

العذر القاهر يرفع إثم الإقامة في بلاد الكفار

(A compelling excuse for lifting the guilt of residency in the Apostate lands)

http://islamweb.net/pls/iweb/fatwa.showSingleFatwa?FatwaId=23444

http://www.abubaseer.bizland.com/books/download/b33.zip

الهِجْرَةُ مسائلٌ .. وأحكام . تأليف : عبد المنعم مصطفى حليمة " أبو بصير "

("Situations and Rulings Associated with *Hijra*" Book by A. M. Halimah)

http://www.islamway.com/arabic/images/lessons//othymeen//mafased1.rm

مفاسد السفر إلى بلاد الكفر . محمد بن صالح العثيمين . الجزء 1

(The Evils of Travel to Apostate Lands, by MBS Al-Uthaimain, Part 1)

http://www.islamway.com/arabic/images/lessons//othymeen//mafased2.rm

مفاسد السفر إلى بلاد الكفر . محمد بن صالح العثيمين . الجزء 2

(The Evils of Travel to Apostate Lands, by MBS Al-Uthaimain, Part 2)

APPENDIX B

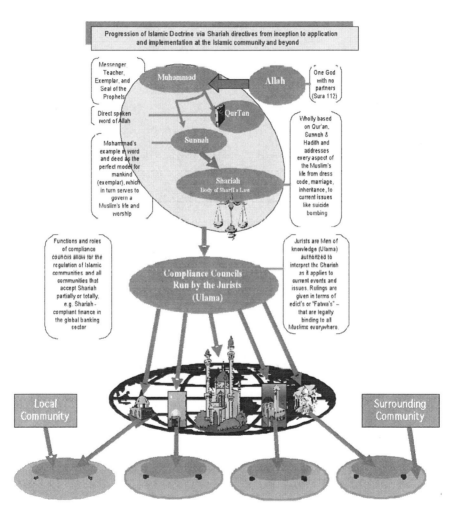

Progression of Islamic Doctrine via Shariah directives from inception to application and implementation at the Islamic community and beyond

Messenger Teacher, Exemplar, and Seal of the Prophets

Muhammad

Allah

One God with no partners (Sura 112)

Direct spoken word of Allah

Qur'an

Wholly based on Qur'an, Sunnah & Hadith and addresses every aspect of the Muslim's life from dress code, marriage, inheritance, to current issues like suicide bombing

Mohammad's example in word and deed as the perfect model for mankind (exemplar), which in turn serves to govern a Muslim's life and worship

Sunnah

Shariah
Body of Shariff's Law

Functions and roles of compliance councils allow for the regulation of Islamic communities and all communities that accept Shariah partially or totally, e.g. Shariah-compliant finance in the global banking sector

Compliance Councils Run by the Jurists (Ulama)

Jurists are Men of knowledge (Ulama) authorized to interpret the Shariah as it applies to current events and issues. Rulings are given in terms of edict's or "Fatwa's" – that are legally binding to all Muslims everywhere.

Local Community

Surrounding Community

CPSIA information can be obtained at www.ICGtesting.com
Printed in the USA
LVOW08s1602050315

429405LV00002B/422/P